CARDINAL NATION

By Rob Rains

Photo credits

R=Right L=Left T=Top B=Bottom M=Middle

Cover Photo: Albert Dickson/The Sporting News
Back Cover: Albert Dickson/The Sporting News
Contents Page:
Page 6 (top to bottom) Peter Newcomb; Peter Newcomb; St. Louis Cardinals; Lewis Portnoy/Spectra-Action, Inc.; Bettmann/Corbis.
Page 7 (top to bottom) Lewis Portnoy/Spectra-Action, Inc.; Albert Dickson/TSN; TSN Archives; Wide World Photos; TSN Archives.

CONTRIBUTING PHOTOGRAPHERS:
Albert Dickson/The Sporting News: 4-5, 8TR, 9, 10-11, 13, 14BL, 16-17, 18, 19, 31, 127,133B, 140B, 147L, 148BL, 150R, 152B, 178TL, 182, 183, 223, 252M, 252B, 253M, 253TR, 253B.
Bob Leverone/The Sporting News: 147R, 222.
Robert Seale/The Sporting News: 6 (background), 144R, 145BR, 148R, 149.
Dilip Vishwanat/The Sporting News: 173R, 173T, 175, 252TR, 253TL.
The Sporting News Archives: 12, 22-25, 28T, 29, 32-42, 45-53, 56-57, 60-65, 78, 80-82, 84, 85TR, 87-89, 91B, 96, 97BR, 99-109, 112-115, 119-121, 125, 130-131, 132L, 134, 136, 139, 141, 142L. 144BL, 145T, 146, 150TL, 153, 153-156, 157L. 157T, 158, 159T, 159BR, 160, 161, 162BL, 162T, 163BR, 165TR, 166L, 168L, 169T, 170L, 171R, 173BL, 176TL,176TR, 177TL, 177M, 177BL, 178BL, 178BR, 178TR, 179M, 179MR, 179TR, 178-179 (background), 184, 185, 189, 190, 191, 196M, 196B, 197T, 200, 201, 208, 209, 216, 217, 218, 219, 221, 225, all photos in The Cardinals Chronology pages 226-253 except as individually noted.
Peter Newcomb: 15, 26-27, 250.
Lewis Portnoy/Spectra-Action, Inc.: 14BR, 28B, 55, 101, 117, 132R, 167M, 167BR, 168T, 169M, 169BL, 170T, 172T, 186.
Allied Photo Color: 159BL, 166R, 176-177 (background), 194T.
Dan Donovan: 95BL, 169BR, 171BL, 171T , 172BL, 254-255.
Malcolm W. Emmons: 205.
Louis Requena/MLB Photos: 54, 58, 59, 110, 111, 116, 118, 124, 162MR, 163TL, 163MR, 164T, 165M, 165BL, 165BR, 167BL.
Rich Pilling/MLB Photos: 67, 68-69, 70, 71T, 71B, 72L, 72R, 73T, 74T, 75, 76TL, 76BL, 77, 123.
NBLA/MLB Photos: 227B.
Photo File/MLB Photos: 8TL, 21, 43.
Photo File: 44, 176BL.
Courtesy of Butch Yatkeman family: 79, 83R, 85B, 157R, 177R.
St. Louis Post-Dispatch: 151, 229T.
Courtesy of St. Louis Cardinals: 122, 179BR, 248T.
Bettmann/Corbis: 86, 87, 92, 93TR, 95TR, 95MR, 96L, 97TL, 97ML, 97TR, 128-129, 164BL, 188B, 188-189, 192, 193, 195, 196TR, 197B, 204, 206, 207, 210, 213, 220, 245TL.
World Wide Photos: 14T, 28TL, 30, 90, 91TL, 91TR, 93TL, 94, 133T, 135T, 143, 181, 187, 194B, 198, 199, 203, 211, 214, 215, 215B, 220T.

ISBN: 0-89204-687-2

Acknowledgements

Some of the details of the first big-league ballgame I attended are a bit hazy now. I don't remember the precise date or year—though I've narrowed it down to 1970 or 1971—and I don't remember the outcome. This, though, I do remember: Shea Stadium, Cardinals and Mets, Gibson and Seaver.

All of 8 or 9 years old, I had always been a Cardinals fan by association; my parents were natives of St. Louis, but through a series of corporate transfers, we rooted for them in Houston, in Chicago and in New York. But on that day at Shea, seeing Gibson and Brock, even from the far reaches of the upper deck, in their bright Cardinal red, I became my own Cardinal fan.

Thirty years of ballgames and memories have been stored away now—Torre, Simmons, the Mad Hungarian, McBride, Herr, Tudor, Jack Clark, McGee, McGwire, Pujols—only adding to the unbridled passion I have for the team.

It's with that unbridled passion that I, and most of the team associated with this book, have compiled this project. It is a project from Cardinals fans, to Cardinals fans and for Cardinals fans. I'm sure a lot of our fondest memories will be among your fondest memories.

I'd like to thank our team for their memories, and more tangible assistance: Rob Rains and Joe Hoppel, the writer and editor who were the workhorses for this project; the design group of Bob Parajon, Michael Behrens, Matt Kindt, Chad Painter, Chris Callan, Jack Kruyne and Angie Pillman; photo editor Pete Newcomb; the prepress specialists, Steve Romer and Pamela Speh, led by Dave Brickey; to Dave Sloan for his assistance.

To the voting group: John Rawlings, Lesley Hunt, Steve Gietschier, Ron Smith, Rob Rains, Joe Hoppel, Dave Sloan and three special friends of TSN, three big Cardinals fans, Jared Hoffman, Tom Kutz and Sally Stanley, for helping select the greatest Cardinals team, moments and performances of all-time.

Special thanks to Dick Zitzmann and Stan Musial for providing the foreword to the book. There can be no one better than Musial to express what it means to be a Cardinal. Special thanks, too, to Allan Protzel, who allowed us to use the treasure of memorabilia from his uncle, longtime Cardinals equipment manager Butch Yatkeman, throughout this book.

As much fun as this was to produce, it also was a lot of hard work by this talented team of people. But nothing would please this group more than to add another chapter or two on some new World Series championship teams.

Steve Meyerhoff
Editorial Director

CARDINAL NATION

Presented by

The SportingNews

Career
HANK AARON
BABE RUTH
WILLIE MAYS
FRANK ROBINSON
H. KILLEBREW
REGGIE JACKSON
MIKE SCHMIDT
MARK McGWIRE
MICKEY MANTLE
JIMMIE FOXX
573
563
548
AUTOTIRE
CAR CARE CENTERS
Home of the Bottom Line Price
MICHELIN
Budweiser
OFFICIAL

Contents

Foreword

From the very first time I put on a St. Louis Cardinals uniform, I knew I was part of something special. More than 60 years later, I still feel that way about the Cardinals, and I know I am not alone.

This is a baseball team that is built on a great tradition, one that goes back more than 100 years. When I was a rookie on the 1942 Cardinals, we had a spirit that we knew was greater than any one player. We had an attitude that there was no way we were going to lose, and we didn't.

I have seen that attitude on many great Cardinal teams over the years, and with many individual players who have gone on to Hall of Fame careers. It still means something special today to be a Cardinal, and I think all of the players understand that.

It was the feeling that Red Schoendienst and Enos Slaughter experienced—and why they became so upset and emotional when they were traded. Lou Brock and Bob Gibson had it, and so did Ozzie Smith and Mark McGwire. There have been so many great players on the Cardinals over the years, and each and every one of them knew how blessed they were.

St. Louis is a special town, and the fans of the Cardinals also are special. Every time I go to Busch Stadium, I still get a sense that I am part of a large extended family. Baseball is a religion in St. Louis. It has always been that way, and I see no reason why that will ever change.

The players understand that they have a certain responsibility when they become a Cardinal, and if they are not willing to accept that, they don't stay a Cardinal for long. They are out there to honor the tradition of the team, to respect the great players who have come before them and to set a standard for future players to follow.

There is something different about wearing a Cardinal uniform, and the different expectations of the fans who follow those players. They know the game, they understand the game, but most important, they love the game. And they love the Cardinals. You can't teach that. It has to come from the heart.

The Cardinals have had great owners over the years, from Sam Breadon to Gussie Busch to the current partners, led by Bill DeWitt. They have all understood the relationship this city has with the Cardinals, and they have accepted their responsibility of always trying to put the best team possible on the field.

Even in the years when the Cardinals didn't win, the fans stuck with them.

There is no greater rivalry in sports than the Cardinals and Cubs, and it doesn't matter if the game is at Busch Stadium or at Wrigley Field. Fans from both teams will pack the place, and it will be jumping.

I was fortunate to play for the Cardinals for 22 years, and I experienced a lot of great moments in my career. My memories of those days are special. I know how lucky I was, and a day doesn't go by when I don't appreciate everything that has happened to me.

That is the attitude all Cardinals should have. Every day they get to walk into that locker room and put on the birds-on-the-bat jersey, they should realize how lucky they are and say a special thank you to whoever was responsible for them being there.

Believe me, there is no better feeling in the world.

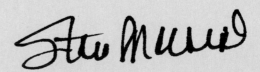

The Essence of the Cardinals

Red Schoendienst and Stan Musial have earned special places in Cardinals
ore, endearing themselves to fans with their many accomplishments on the
field and their fan-friendly approach to the game. Still, star players—and great
eams—are only a part of the st◼◼ed history of the St. Louis franchise.

Part of the beauty of baseball is that you never know what's going to happen. You could see a no-hitter or a triple play. Someone could hit four home runs. The game could last 20 innings.

In the history of the St. Louis Cardinals, all of those things—and much more—have happened. But mere results, the wins and losses, the record-setting performances—they don't tell the whole history of this team.

The essence of the Cardinals, a storied National League franchise that traces its lineage to 1892, can be found in the people who have been part of the organization. Some of the most notable players in the game's history—Dizzy Dean, Frankie Frisch, Enos Slaughter, Stan Musial, Bob Gibson and Mark McGwire, to name a few—have worn the famous birds-on-the-bat logo.

The 1930s Gas House Gang is among the most celebrated teams in baseball history. Rogers Hornsby batted over .400 three times. Ozzie Smith was a Gold Glove magician, a player whose induction into the Hall of Fame in July 2002 will mark the 38th time that an enshrinee has had a Cardinals connection.

Great players, managers and executives have helped make the Cardinals a legendary franchise—but so, too, have little-known front-office people, scouts, minor league operatives and men and women associated with the club in obscure capacities. They have labored long and hard, often without recognition, because of their love of the game.

George Kissell has worked for the Cardinals for more than 60 years—as a minor league player, manager and instructor, and as a coach on the major league level. He has spent many a night on steamy fields in Johnson City, Tenn., St. Petersburg, Fla., and Little Rock, Ark. He has helped shape the careers of countless Cardinals—from Mike Shannon to Joe Torre to Ted Simmons to Todd Zeile to Placido Polanco.

What the players learned from Kissell—and great teachers like him—was the Cardinal Way of playing baseball.

"George is a fundamental person," Simmons said. "He teaches A, B, C and D. He won't give it to you any other way. And he won't go to B until he's convinced that you understand A. As far as teaching me fundamentals and an understanding of the way the game is played, George has had more impact on me than any person I've met or known."

Added Torre: "When I got to the Cardinals and met up with George Kissell, (that's) when I found out how the game should be played. The man is tireless. He cares, that's the biggest thing. He'll yell and scream at you, but it's like your mom or

Enos Slaughter was reduced to tears in April 1954 after learning he no longer would be wearing a Cardinals uniform. Slaughter had just been traded to the New York Yankees.

dad yelling. You don't like them yelling at you, but you know they're doing it because they love you."

Although Kissell and other minor league instructors are an integral part of the essence of the Cardinals, they aren't the complete story, either.

The revolutionary farm system itself is a key component of the Cardinals' rich history—and success. Created by Branch Rickey in the 1920s, it put the Cards far ahead of other teams in the signing and development of talent. The farm chain had as many as 25 teams at one point.

Cardinals baseball means tradition—a tradition passed on not only by the skills of the players, but by word of mouth. In back yards and on front porches throughout the Midwest, South and Southwest, Cardinals games have been heard for decades over the team's far-flung radio network. The smell of barbecue has mixed with

Cardinals baseball means the broadcasting excellence of Jack Buck, the longtime ownership of the franchise by August A. "Gussie" Busch Jr. (middle photo, throwing out the first pitch, with son August Busch III standing nearby) and the presence of such Hall of Famers as Bob Gibson, Stan Musial, Red Schoendienst and Lou Brock.

the voices of France Laux, Harry Caray, Jack Buck and Mike Shannon.

The Cardinals were one of the first teams to recognize the power of radio. Through the magic of such talents as Caray and Buck, millions of listeners have been transformed into Cardinals fans.

The love of the Cardinals is handed down from generation to generation, just like grandma's diamond ring and the family Bible. Grandfathers tell what it was like watching Musial and other standout players at old Sportsman's Park. Their sons tell their children about watching Gibson and Lou Brock. This generation will tell sons and daughters about September 8, 1998, the date Big Mac pushed Roger Maris out of the record book.

This love affair does more than generate affection. It also educates, making fans in the stands and those at home appreciate such fundamental skills as advancing a runner to second base with a ground ball to the right side. Clearly, the fans' knowledge of the finer points of the game has contributed to St. Louis' billing as one of the best baseball cities in America— if not the very best.

You see it at parks and playgrounds across the city and throughout the region. Kids are wearing McGwire, Jim Edmonds and Albert Pujols jerseys. In pickup games, every kid wants his team to be the Cardinals. No one wants to be the Cubs. Or the Dodgers. Or even the Yankees.

Because of their understanding and appreciation of the game, St. Louis fans cheer the deeds of both superstars and bench players. When third-string catcher Glenn Brummer stole home in a game in 1982, it was a moment to cherish. It still is. When

On game day, Busch Stadium is always awash in a sea of red. The ballpark opened in May 1966.

Mike Laga hit a foul ball out of Busch Stadium in 1986—no batted ball of any kind had ever left the stadium's confines—there was a buzz in the crowd. Fans realized they had just witnessed a first.

Many of those same fans went crazy when Ozzie Smith homered in the 1985 National League Championship Series, just as Jack Buck told them to do. And the fans booed umpire Don Denkinger in the '85 World Series, even if the catcalls emanated from

their living rooms.

Although particularly attached to longtime Cardinals players, St. Louis fans also hold some short-termers in high esteem—players like Cesar Cedeno and Will Clark, late-season acquisitions who helped the Cards reach the playoffs in 1985 and 2000, respectively.

Fans have cheered Jose Oquendo and Rex Hudler and Joe McEwing, not because they were great players, but because they played the game at warp

speed, diving for balls, sliding headfirst. It's the Cardinal Way.

It's the way the Gas House Gang went about its business. It's the feisty Orlando Cepeda-led "El Birdos" of 1967. It's Whiteyball. It's Slaughter crying after being told he no longer would wear the birds on the bat—he had just been traded to the Yankees.

It, again, is tradition.

When pitcher Bob Shirley joined the Cardinals in a trade from San Diego after the 1980 season, he

sized up the difference in atmospheres. "Here, tradition is Stan Musial and Bob Gibson and Lou Brock walking into the clubhouse," he said. "In San Diego, it was (former Padres star) Nate Colbert trying to sell you a used car."

The tradition was what McGwire noticed and quickly came to appreciate after he arrived from Oakland. Edmonds sensed it, too. And young guys like J.D. Drew and Matt Morris feel it as well.

"It wasn't until I got to St. Louis that I really got to

With the franchise's standout players clearly on a pedestal, Busch Stadium-bound fans can steal a look at the statues of Lou Brock and other notable Cardinals.

"When the baseball season starts in St. Louis, they bleed (Cardinal) red."
—Mark McGwire

know and understand the passion fans here have for baseball," McGwire said. "When the baseball season starts in St. Louis, they bleed (Cardinal) red. Everybody told me I'd love St. Louis, and no wonder."

Smith, the Cardinals' newest Hall of Famer and one of St. Louis' most-loved citizens, understands exactly what McGwire means.

"This town has such a rich baseball history, you can't help but be caught up in it," Smith said during his playing days. "They're all here, all the great ones. Musial, (Marty) Marion, (Red) Schoendienst, Gibson. They're people you see all the time, people you can reach out and touch. And the memories of others, like the Deans, are still here, too.

"Everything here seems to come full circle back to the ballpark. I feel I'm part of, well, a common cause."

That cause is St. Louis Cardinals baseball.

Hall *of* Fame
LEGENDS

SMIRE *Ozzie*

The back flips. The horizontal leaps. The unlikely home run. Those are the thoughts that first come to mind when you think of Ozzie Smith.

The somersaults came as Smith ran onto the field before a season-opening game, or a playoff game, or a World Series game. The diving plays were at shortstop, where Ozzie would follow his acrobatics by somehow plucking the ball out of the air. The homer was against the Dodgers' Tom Niedenfuer and won a pivotal National League Championship Series game.

Yet those mental freeze-frame images do not provide a complete picture of who Smith was as a player or what made him perhaps the greatest fielding shortstop in baseball history.

Career stats:
.978 fielding pct.
2,460 hits
580 stolen bases

2002

Highlights: Hall of Fame Class 2002 ... 13-time Gold Glove winner ... Led the league eight times in fielding percentage, seven times as a Cardinal ... Played in 14 All-Star Games.

To capture the complete image of Smith, you have to go back to the early 1960s, when he was a young boy growing up in the Watts section of Los Angeles. When he didn't have anyone to play catch with, he played by himself, either bouncing a ball off the concrete steps of his house, each time trying to make a better catch than the time before, or throwing the ball off the roof of his home, each time attempting to make a more spectacular diving grab.

Smith dreamed the same dreams as millions of young boys—he wanted to be a major leaguer. The difference was that Smith didn't merely dream the dream, he worked to make the dream a reality.

He took pride in himself and in his accomplishments. He knew he wasn't the most physically gifted player. He knew other guys were bigger and stronger, hit the ball harder and farther and threw it with more velocity. He didn't talk about what he couldn't do; instead, he concentrated on what he could do—play shortstop.

The other skills, especially on offense, had to be developed later, even after he reached the major leagues. When he was acquired by the Cardinals from San Diego in an early-1982 trade for fellow shortstop Garry Templeton, one of the first things Smith did was accept a bet from manager Whitey Herzog. For every ground ball or line drive that Smith hit, Herzog would

pay him a dollar. Every time Smith flied out or struck out, he had to pay Herzog a dollar.

Herzog called off the bet by the middle of Smith's first season in St. Louis because he could tell Smith grasped what he needed to do to become successful offensively.

Herzog and others marveled at Smith's defense, though everyone knew he would be very good afield. Good enough, it turned out, to win 13 consecutive Gold Gloves. Herzog often credited Smith's defense—his glove saved a run or two per game, some experts thought—with providing as much help for his team as a hitter with sizable run-production numbers.

Smith was rewarded financially. He became the first player to be paid more on the basis of what he did defensively than offensively.

A wizard with the glove, Ozzie Smith made himself into a good hitter. Under Whitey Herzog's tutelage, he quickly grasped what he needed to do to improve offensively.

FIELDING PERCENTAGE
.978

Smith's acrobatic skills made it possible for him to knock down balls that most shortstops couldn't reach. He also had the uncanny ability to bounce back up and make the throw—with time to spare.

It had been a cliche since not long after the game's inception that teams won with pitching and defense, but Smith made it more than just a saying upon joining the Cardinals. In his first season with St. Louis, he proved emphatically that it was true.

It was the team success of the Cardinals that made the baseball world notice how valuable Smith was because of his defense. The Cards won the World Series in 1982, Ozzie's initial year with the team, and they captured National League pennants in 1985 and 1987.

It was ironic, then, that one of the greatest moments in Ozzie Smith's career came on offense. With the Cardinals and Dodgers tied at two victories apiece in the 1985 NLCS, Smith slugged a game-winning home run off Niedenfuer in the ninth inning of Game 5. Remarkably, it was his first career homer batting lefthanded, coming in his 2,968th at-bat from that side of the plate.

Smith used the dramatic moment as an opportunity to answer critics who had doubted his ability over the years.

Smith's homer in the 1985 NLCS drove home the point that he could handle the bat.

"I'm not supposed to be able to hit," Smith said. "But if I listened to all of those things, I wouldn't be in the position I am now. You've got to believe in yourself. I've always been taught you only get out of something what you put into it. I'm always going to have skeptics. This isn't going to change anything. This is the way it's been my whole career."

Actually, the home run did help convince some of the remaining doubters that Smith was, in fact, a pretty good offensive player. He could run, steal bases. And even if he didn't hit more than two or three home runs a year, that wasn't his job and wasn't what he was being paid to do.

Much like a Cardinals Hall of Famer from a previous generation, Lou Brock, Smith was viewed as a one-dimensional player. Brock was known as a basestealer, but he still wound up with more than 3,000 hits. Smith finished his career with 2,460. Through sheer hard work, the Wizard, who had hit .222 the season before he was traded to St. Louis, posted such season batting averages as .280, .303, .285, .295 and .288 for the Cardinals.

When he retired after the 1996

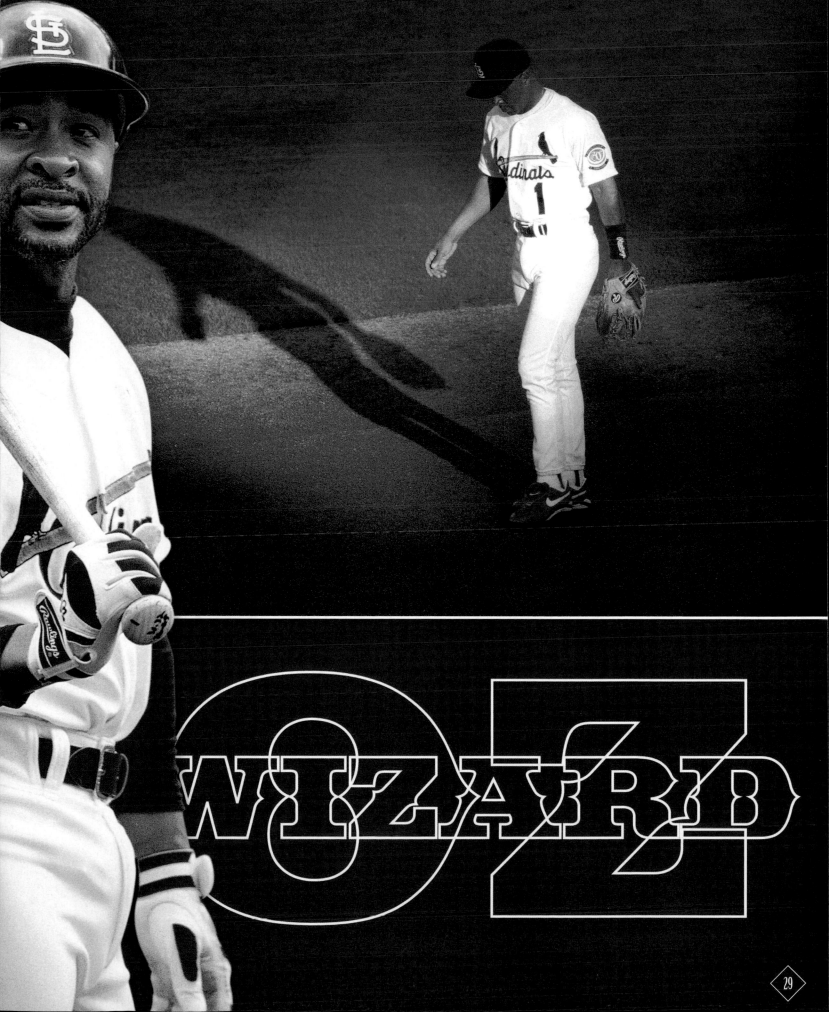

WIZARD OF OZ

season at age 41, Smith had received more all-time votes for the All-Star Game than any player in National League history. He played in 14 All-Star Games and was selected another time but didn't play because of injury. He owned seven major league fielding records for short-stops, including career marks for assists and double plays. He also owned numerous single-season records, including the National League mark for fewest errors in a season, eight, set in 1991 (and since broken).

Smith played much of his career with a torn rotator cuff, but he never underwent surgery because he didn't want to be sidelined for the extensive period required for recovery. To compensate, he made adjustments in the way he positioned himself on defense and the manner in which he threw the ball. Not many people even knew about the injury—thus there was little appreciation for the subtle-but-crucial changes he made in his game.

Smith retired knowing he had provided the leadership and dedication to the game that was expected of him by others—and by Ozzie himself. He was like an older brother to such young players as Willie McGee, Vince Coleman and Terry Pendleton, and his mentoring and guidance no doubt played a major role in those players' individual success—and in the Cardinals' collective success.

When Smith reflected on his career, he was satisfied.

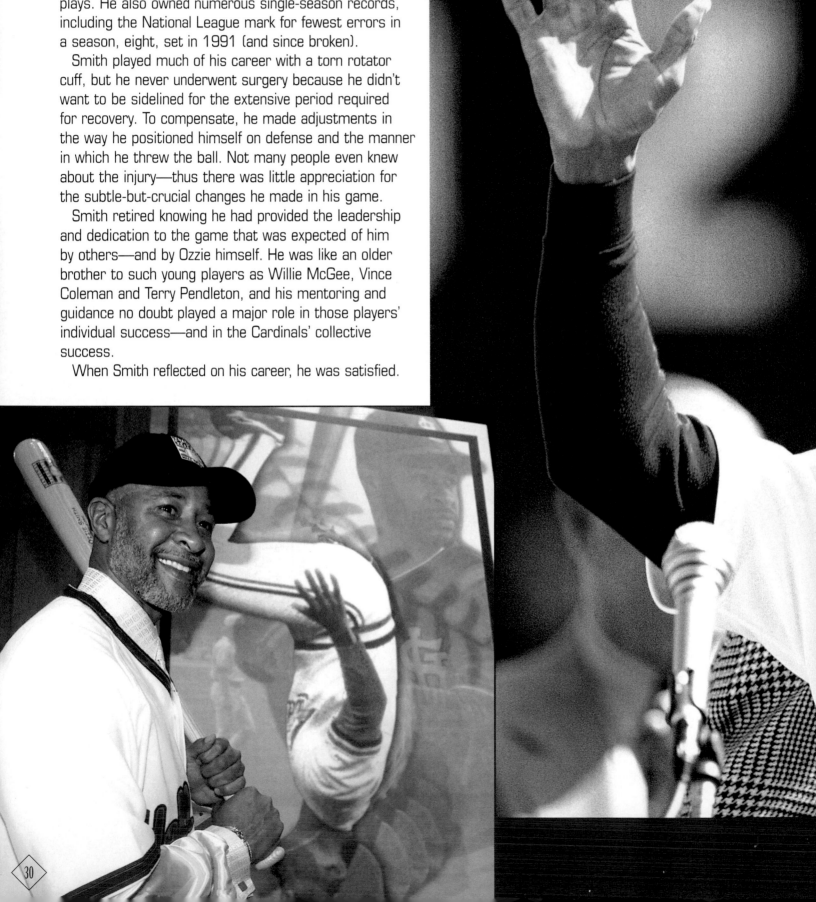

Honored in St. Louis (above) as his career wound down, Smith received baseball's ultimate tribute in 2002 when he was voted into the Hall of Fame. He wore a Hall jersey to note the occasion.

"I've always worked hard at everything I've done. All you can try to do is work hard every day and get the maximum out of what it is you possess. I think I've done that."

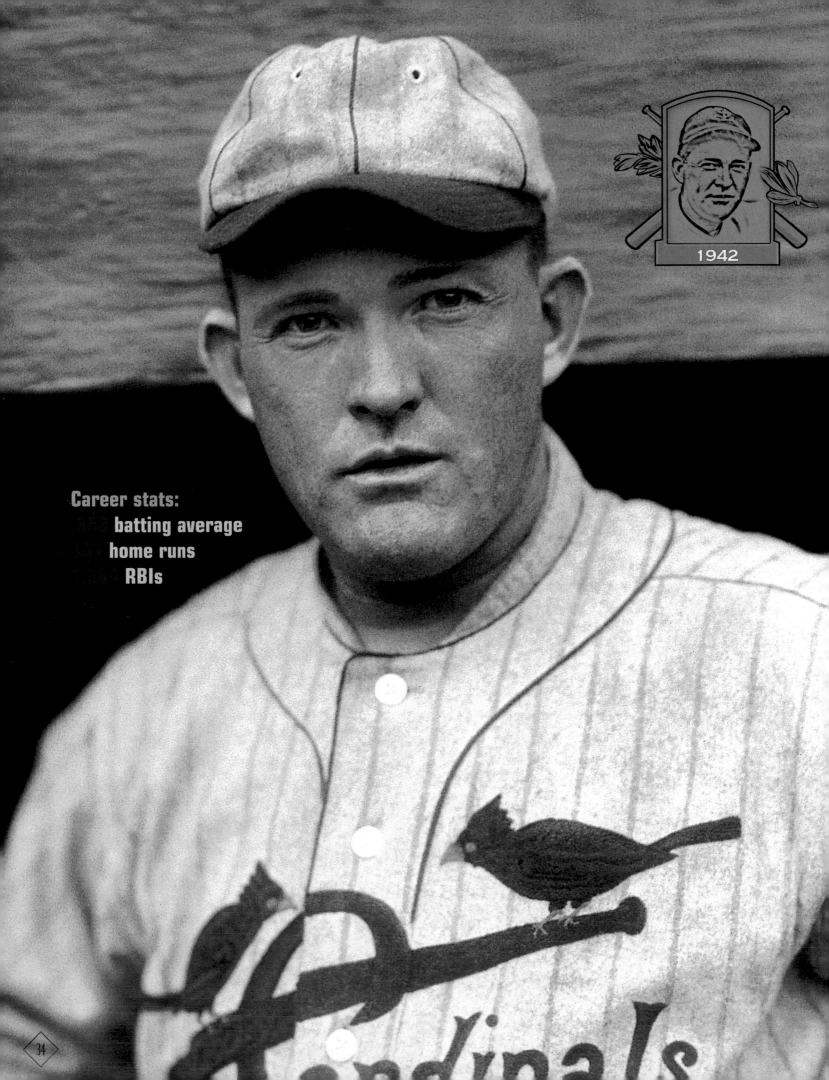

Career stats:
.XXX batting average
XXX home runs
X,XXX RBIs

1942

34

POSITION 2nd base　　　**CARDINALS SEASONS** 1915-26, 1933

When Cardinals manager Miller Huggins told a 135-pound youngster named Rogers Hornsby that he was not big enough for the major leagues, it meant the infielder was being farmed out—but not in the manner known nowadays.

Hornsby spent the winter of 1915-16 working on his uncle's farm, and he added 25 pounds of muscle to his frame. When he reported to spring training in 1916 at the ripe old age of 19, he looked like a different player.

Hornsby won a job with the Cardinals and stayed with the club through the 1926 season, becoming one of the most-feared hitters in the game. He won the Triple Crown twice, captured six consecutive batting titles, topped the .400 mark three times in four years and was the manager/second baseman for the Cardinals' first World Series champion, the '26 team. He would say years later that despite all of his offensive exploits, his greatest baseball thrill was tagging out Babe Ruth to end the '26 Series. Ruth was attempting to steal second base, but catcher Bob O'Farrell threw him out.

Never one to shy away from a confrontation, Hornsby was often at odds with Cardinals owner Sam Breadon. But news after the '26 season that Hornsby had been traded to the Giants for Frankie Frisch still left St. Louis fans shaken.

Highlights: Considered the greatest righthanded hitter of all time ... His .424 average in 1924 was the majors' best in the 20th century ... Had 250 hits in 1922 after collecting 235 the year before ... In one five-year span, he hit .402 ... Also played for Giants, Braves, Cubs and Browns.

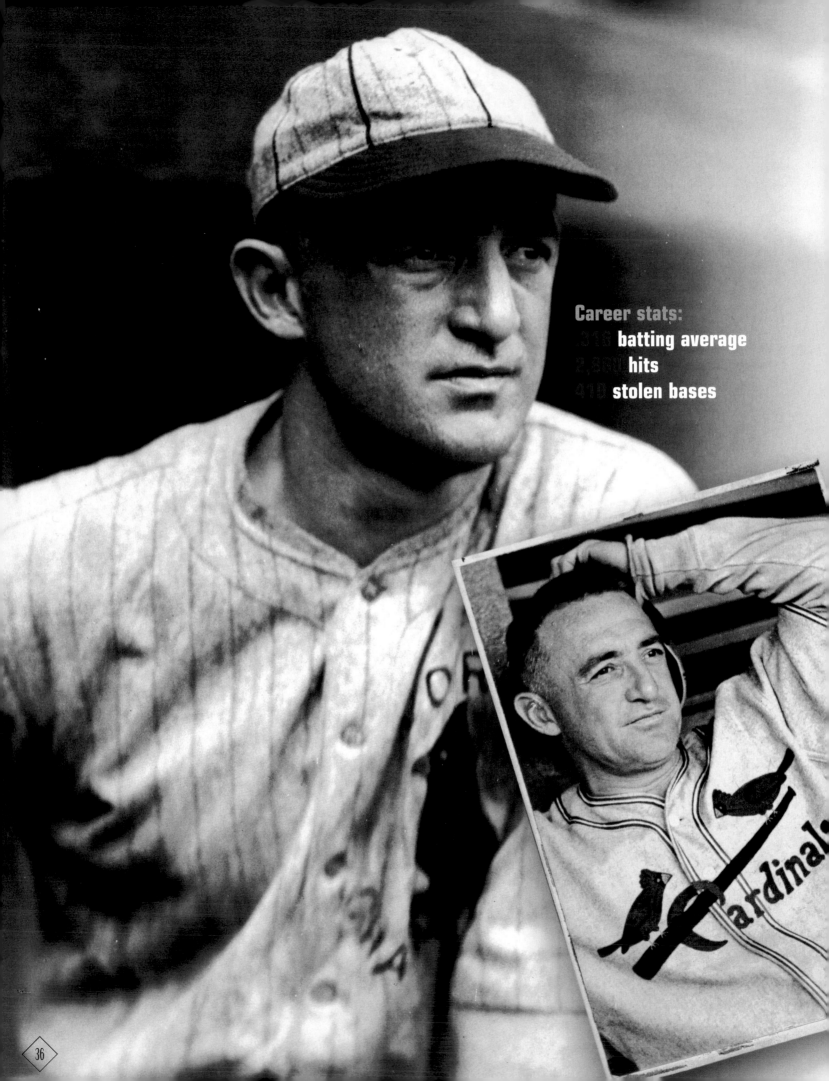

Career stats:
.31? batting average
2,8?? hits
41? stolen bases

FRISCH
Frankie

Trading one of the game's greatest players is never a popular move. Cardinals owner Sam Breadon was heavily criticized—and then some—after dealing second baseman/manager Rogers Hornsby to the New York Giants in December 1926—10 weeks after the Cards had won their first World Series championship. St. Louis got second baseman Frankie Frisch and so-so pitcher Jimmy Ring for Hornsby, who had batted .400-plus three times for the Cardinals.

When Frisch had a bad day defensively in his first exhibition game in a Cardinals uniform, the attacks only intensified. Frisch proceeded to calm St. Louis fans' fears with a spectacular 1927 season, and he wound up playing 11 years in St. Louis—a stint during which he managed the team in its Gas House Gang era.

Highly educated and possessing a multitude of interests besides baseball, Frisch was a fiery competitor. He was frequently at odds with more relaxed players—some of whom didn't always take the game as seriously as Frisch, a man who had no time for those who committed mental mistakes, questioned his authority or failed to give 100 percent.

As it turned out, Hornsby made the Hall of Fame in 1942. Frisch was enshrined in 1947, after hitting above .325 eight times in his 19-year major league career, winning three National League stolen base titles and managing the 1934 Cardinals to a World Series crown.

It wasn't such a bad trade after all, Mr. Breadon.

Highlights: N.L. MVP in 1931, when he batted .311 with 82 RBIs and a league-high 28 steals ... Hit the first N.L. home run in All-Star Game history, connecting in the inaugural game in 1933 ... Managed the Cardinals from 1933 to 1938, guiding the Gas House Gang to the 1934 World Series title.

1947

DEAN

Dizzy

Never has a player had a more appropriate nickname than Jay Hanna Dean, the man known as "Dizzy."

When he was pitching in the minor leagues in St. Joseph, Mo., Dean had rooms booked at three hotels so he could stay wherever it was most convenient. In Philadelphia, he and a few Cardinals teammates donned overalls and acted like construction workers as they interrupted a banquet. And, the story goes, he once walked a hitter with two out in the ninth inning so he could pitch to Bill Terry. Dizzy walked in from the mound and told Terry he had promised some hospitalized kids he would strike out Terry that day. He did, too.

Dean always said it wasn't bragging if you could back up your words. After he threw a three-hit shutout at Brooklyn in the first game of a doubleheader in 1934, he watched brother Paul throw a no-hitter in the nightcap. Diz said that if he had known Paul was going to pitch a no-hitter, he would have hurled one, too.

By the time he was 25 years old, Dean had won 121 games in the majors, led the National League in strikeouts four times and twice topped the league in wins. In '34 he went 30-7. He remains the last National Leaguer to win 30 games in one season.

After breaking a toe in the 1937 All-Star Game, Dean altered his pitching motion and suffered an arm injury. He never won a game after age 29. But he had made his mark, with his swagger and his arm. His career winning percentage: .644.

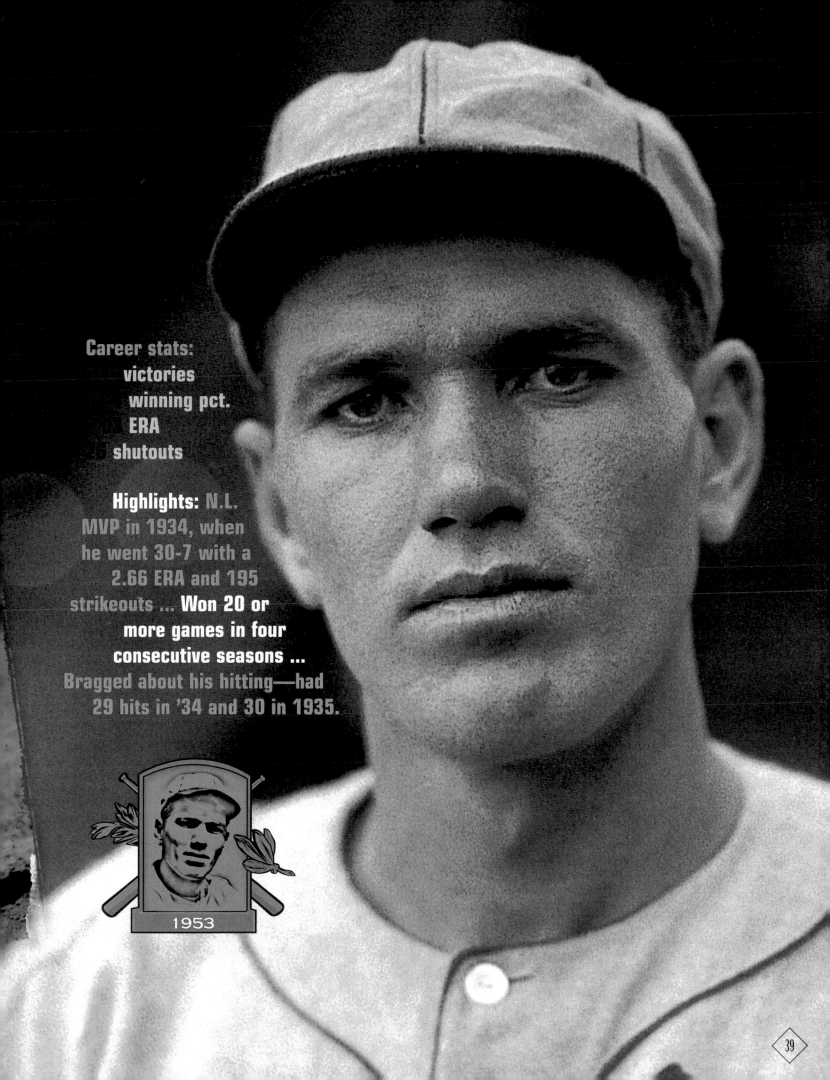

Career stats:
victories
winning pct.
ERA
shutouts

Highlights: N.L. MVP in 1934, when he went 30-7 with a 2.66 ERA and 195 strikeouts ... **Won 20 or more games in four consecutive seasons ...** Bragged about his hitting—had 29 hits in '34 and 30 in 1935.

1953

1968

Highlights: Nicknamed "Ducky" for the way he walked ... Won the N.L. Triple Crown in 1937, hitting .374 with 31 home runs and 154 RBIs. Also named N.L. MVP that season ... Played in 10 All-Star Games, six as a Cardinal ... Led the league in RBIs three consecutive years.

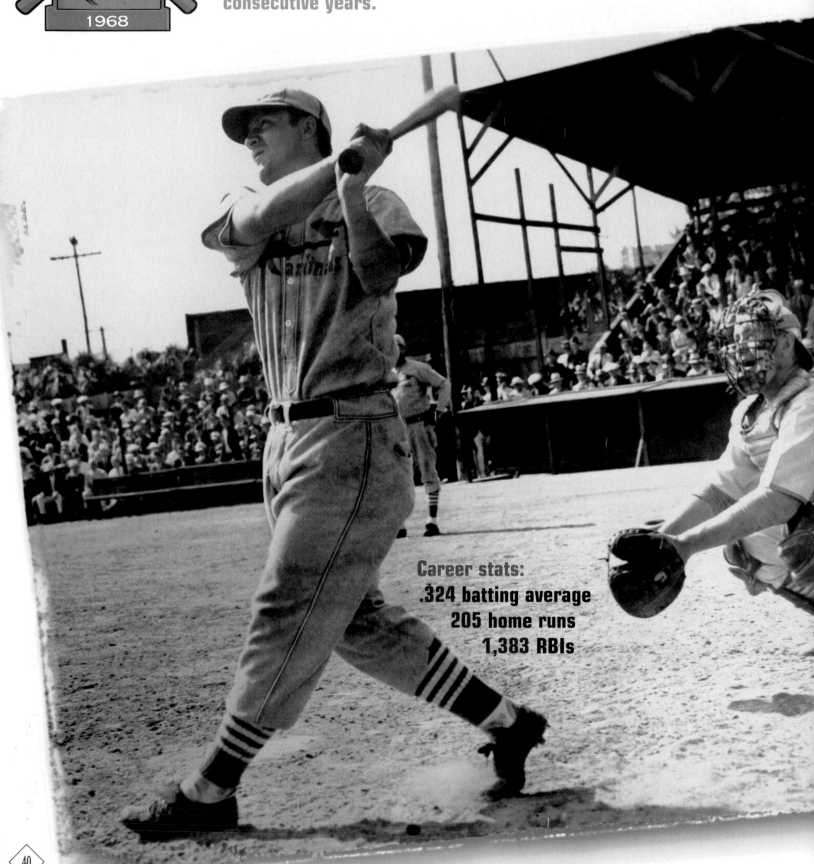

Career stats:
.324 batting average
205 home runs
1,383 RBIs

MEDWICK Joe

Joe Medwick was known primarily for two things during his Cardinals career—his success as a notorious bad-ball hitter and his penchant for never backing down from a fight, even if it meant taking on one or more of his teammates.

After Dizzy Dean and brother Paul once confronted Medwick in the dugout after he misplayed a fly ball into three runs for the opposition, Medwick soon responded with a grand slam. He then spat a mouthful of water at Dizzy's feet and followed with a "Let's see if you can keep that lead" challenge.

Medwick turned down a scholarship to play football at Notre Dame, so there was no questioning his toughness. It was his hard slide into Tigers third baseman Marv Owen that threatened to turn Game 7 of the 1934 World Series into a riot. With the Cardinals on the way to a blowout victory, commissioner Kenesaw Mountain Landis quieted an angry Detroit crowd by ordering Medwick's removal from the game in the sixth inning.

The man known as "Ducky" was an RBI machine for the Cardinals from 1933 through 1939, driving in 861 runs over those seven seasons. He won the Triple Crown in 1937 and remains the last National Leaguer to accomplish that feat.

A Cardinal since 1932, Medwick was traded to the Dodgers in 1940 and also played for the Giants and Braves. Fittingly, he concluded his stellar major league career—he batted .324 over 17 seasons—with the Cardinals, playing sparingly for his old team in 1947 and 1948.

Career stats:
.331 batting average
475 home runs
1,951 RBIs
3,630 hits

1969

Signed to a professional baseball contract out of the mining hills of Pennsylvania when he was only 17 years old, Stan Musial hardly appeared destined to become the greatest player in Cardinals history.

Musial was signed as a pitcher and started out making $65 a month. By his third season in the minors, 1940, he was still in the low reaches of St. Louis' farm system, playing for Daytona Beach of the Class D Florida State League.

In what appeared to be a break-through year, though, Musial compiled an 18-5 record in 28 mound appearances in '40 and, showing a good bat, also saw extensive duty in the outfield. But, late in the season, he suffered a setback: Attempting to make a shoe-string catch, he fell heavily on his left (pitching) shoulder. A knot developed, and Musial wondered if his baseball career was over.

Daytona Beach manager Dickie Kerr, the former White Sox pitcher, persuaded Musial not to quit the game. In the spring of 1941,

Highlights: In 1948, he led the league in all major offensive categories except home runs. Hit .376 with 39 homers and 131 RBIs ... Was N.L. MVP in 1943, 1946 and '48 ... Appeared in 24 All-Star Games, hitting a record six home runs, including a game-winning smash at Milwaukee in 1955 ... On May 2, 1954, he hit five home runs in a doubleheader against the Giants.

Cardinals executive Branch Rickey and his lieutenant, Burt Shotton, talked manager Ollie Vanek into taking Musial on his roster as an outfielder for the Cards' Class C team in Springfield, Mo.

Success followed immediately. Musial began hitting the ball for average and power, and he rose from Springfield to Rochester of the International League as the season wore on. By the end of September, he found himself in the major leagues, where he batted .426 for the Cardinals in 12 games.

Excluding one year in military service, Musial proceeded to hit line drives for the next 21 seasons. Along the way, he won seven National League batting titles.

By the time he retired in 1963, after collecting career hit No. 3,630 in his last at-bat and finishing with a .331 life-time batting average, Musial was recognized as one of game's all-time elite players. His nickname, "Stan the Man," had come by way of Brooklyn, where fans moaned every time they saw "that man" coming to the plate. Musial hit well everywhere, but he found cozy Ebbets Field particularly inviting.

Musial won three N.L. Most Valuable Player awards, captured his first batting title in 1943 at age 22 and his last in 1957, when he was 36. He led the N.L. in doubles eight times, was tops in triples five times and was No. 1 in runs scored five times. Even though he was never considered a top-of-the-line home run hitter, he finished just 25 homers shy of the coveted 500 mark.

He missed the Triple Crown by only one home run in 1948 (a year in which he batted .376, hit 39 homers and drove in 131 runs). Never one to complain about such matters, Musial exhibited a grace and friendliness throughout his career that endeared him more to teammates and fans than his baseball skill did—and that is saying a lot. After all, with a bat in his hand, the Cardinals' Stan Musial was truly "The Man."

HAINES Jesse

POSITION Pitcher   UNIFORM NO 16   CARDINALS SEASONS 1920-37

When Jesse Haines began losing some of the zip on his fastball, he knew he had to come up with another pitch if he wanted to stay in the major leagues.

That pitch was a knuckleball, taught to him by Philadelphia A's righthander Ed Rommel. It was different than the knuckleball of the modern era, because the ball actually was gripped with the knuckles, not the fingertips. The pitch acted more like a spitball and didn't flutter.

Haines was the starting pitcher in Game 7 of the 1926 World Series, and he limited the Yankees to two runs through 6⅔ innings before a sore finger (the result of his knuckleball grip rubbing away some skin) and a mounting New York threat forced him out of the game. Grover Cleveland Alexander came on in relief and struck out Tony Lazzeri with the bases loaded. Six outs later, the Cardinals were World Series champions for the first time.

One of Haines' most memorable games came in a losing effort against Alexander and the Cubs in Jesse's rookie season, 1920. He and Alexander both went the distance in a 17-inning game that Chicago won, 3-2. Haines didn't allow a hit from the seventh inning through the 16th.

In 1924, Haines pitched the first no-hitter in Cardinals history, shutting down the Boston Braves, 5-0, at Sportsman's Park.

Haines spent 18 years with the Cardinals, the longest pitching tenure in club history, and he won 210 games, second on the Cards' all-time list to Bob Gibson's 251.

1970

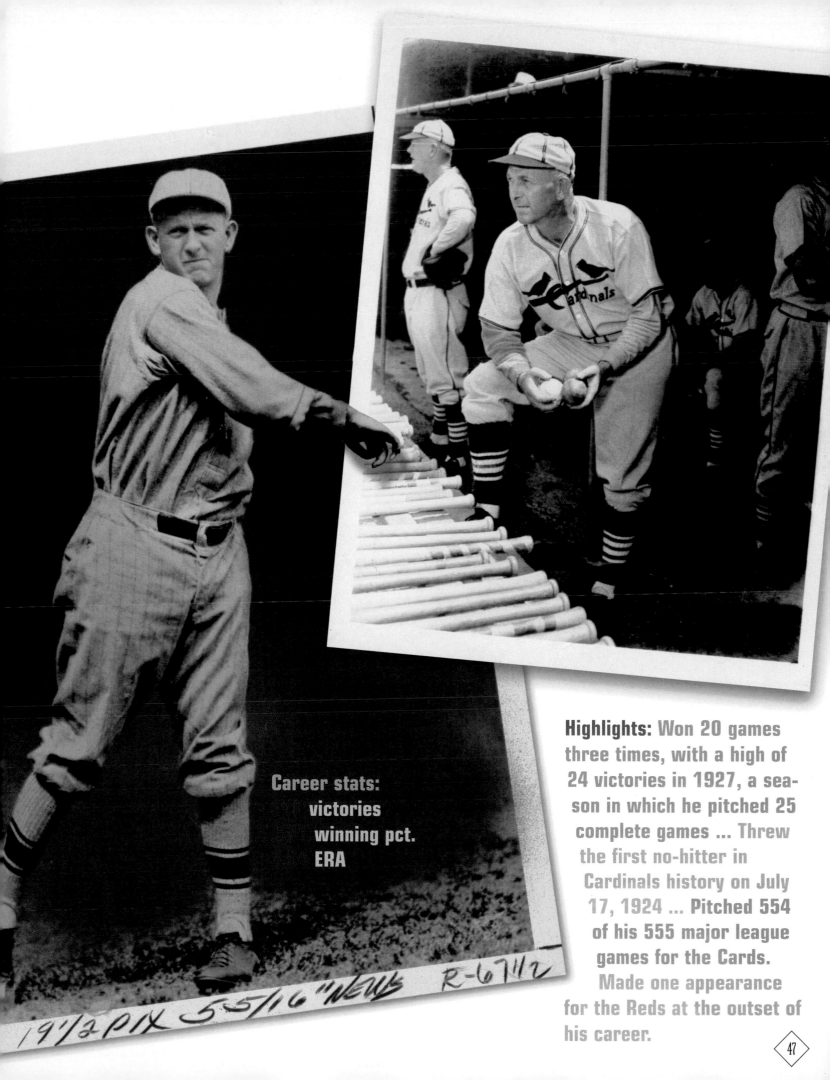

Career stats:
victories
winning pct.
ERA

Highlights: Won 20 games three times, with a high of 24 victories in 1927, a season in which he pitched 25 complete games ... Threw the first no-hitter in Cardinals history on July 17, 1924 ... Pitched 554 of his 555 major league games for the Cards. Made one appearance for the Reds at the outset of his career.

47

HAFEY Chick

Chick Hafey's career statistics are impressive by any yardstick. But when you consider that Hafey performed at a Hall of Fame level despite serious vision problems, his accomplishments are downright amazing.

Branch Rickey, one of the best judges of talent in the game's history, believed that Hafey—if blessed with normal eyesight and good health—might have become the best righthanded hitter baseball had ever known.

Beaned several times during the 1926 season (when he was 23 years old), Hafey began wearing glasses on a doctor's recommendation. He had so much trouble with his eyes that he had three pair of glasses, with different prescriptions, and the outfielder selected his eyewear depending on how his vision was on a particular day. His sight also was affected by a serious sinus condition.

Teammates said that on bad days, Hafey had trouble making out the red "Exit" sign on a railroad car.

Despite his physical problems, Hafey won the National League batting title in 1931, edging the Giants' Bill Terry and Cardinals teammate Jim Bottomley, and in the process he led the Cardinals to their fourth pennant in six years.

Amid a contract dispute, Hafey, a .326 hitter over eight seasons with St. Louis, was traded to the Reds in April 1932. Poor vision continued to hamper him, and by 1937—at age 34—he was playing his final season in the majors.

Highlights: Won the N.L. batting title in 1931 with a .349 mark. Was the tightest race ever, Hafey finishing at .3489, the Giants' Bill Terry at .3486 and Cards teammate Jim Bottomley at .348 ... Hit .336 or higher four straight seasons.

1971

Career stats:
.317 batting average
164 home runs
833 RBIs

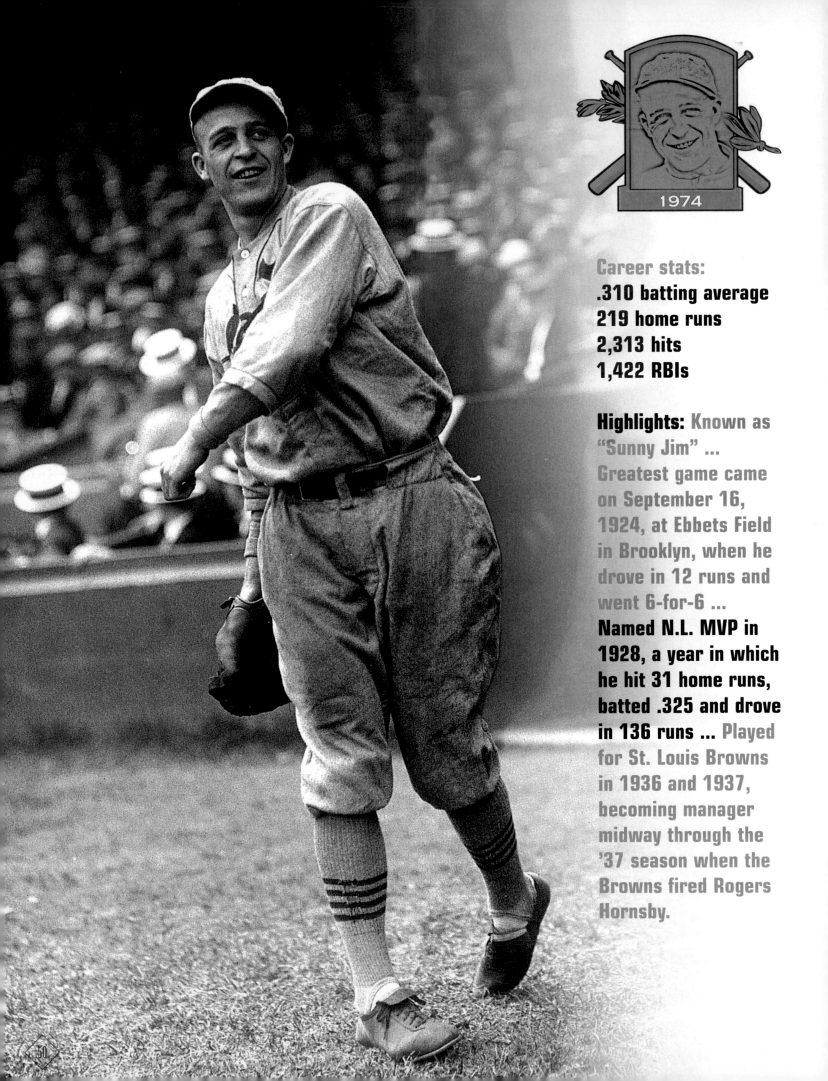

1974

Career stats:
.310 batting average
219 home runs
2,313 hits
1,422 RBIs

Highlights: Known as "Sunny Jim" ... Greatest game came on September 16, 1924, at Ebbets Field in Brooklyn, when he drove in 12 runs and went 6-for-6 ... **Named N.L. MVP in 1928, a year in which he hit 31 home runs, batted .325 and drove in 136 runs ...** Played for St. Louis Browns in 1936 and 1937, becoming manager midway through the '37 season when the Browns fired Rogers Hornsby.

50

POSITION 1st base   **UNIFORM NO** 4   **CARDINALS SEASONS** 1922-32

It was the promise and the eventual success of such young players as Jim Bottomley that convinced Branch Rickey to develop players through a network of minor league affiliates.

At age 19, Bottomley was playing semipro ball in Illinois and working as a blacksmith apprentice when he was discovered and signed by a Cardinals scout. Three years later, in 1922, he was playing first base in the major leagues.

Rickey figured that by controlling and grooming his own players from the days they entered the pro ranks, he would have the edge on teams that signed and purchased players merely as opportunities arose. And by the time Bottomley (just the kind of young player Rickey envisioned) was in his third full season in the majors, Rickey had an eight-team farm system in place.

As for the career of the man known as "Sunny" because of his easygoing disposition, there was a lot to smile about during Bottomley's 11 seasons with the Cardinals. He drove in 111 or more runs for six consecutive years and won the National League's MVP award in 1928. He also played on the Cardinals' first World Series championship team and their first four pennant-winning clubs.

Other players smiled when they were around Bottomley—not just because of his lusty hitting, but also because of his naivete. Early in his career, he noticed a long, slender bat in the dugout rack. Turning to a veteran pitcher, he asked, "Pardon me, sir, but who is this Mr. Fungo?"

The biggest smile on Bottomley's face came on September 16, 1924, when he established a major league record by driving in 12 runs in one game (a mark tied 69 years later by another Cardinals player, Mark Whiten). Bottomley's big day—he went 6-for-6 against Brooklyn at Ebbets Field—featured a grand slam and a two-run homer. He also had a run-scoring double and three singles that knocked in five runs.

Career stats:

.312 batting average
359 home runs
1,337 RBIs

Two leg injuries almost ended Johnny Mize's major league career before it began. Mize "retired" in 1935, his sixth minor league season, but the parent Cardinals weren't convinced he should give up the game. Cards executives summoned Mize to St. Louis for a medical examination.

Dr. Robert F. Hyland, the team physician, diagnosed the injury as bone spurs and performed an operation. Because he couldn't play every day in 1936 until fully recovered from surgery, Mize remained in St. Louis with the thought that he could see occasional duty as a Cardinals pinch hitter.

When his legs healed, Mize settled in as the Cards' first baseman and had six stellar seasons ('36 through 1941) with St. Louis. He drove in 653 runs and captured a National League batting title in that span. His 43 home runs in 1940 led the majors and stood as the Cardinals' single-season record until the mark was broken by Mark McGwire in 1998.

Mize, who was traded to the New York Giants in December 1941 and had a 51-homer season for the Giants six years later, earned the nickname "Big Cat" for his defensive abilities at first base, but he is remembered more for his offensive exploits. In Cardinals history, only three players have led the league at least once in batting average, doubles, triples and home runs—Rogers Hornsby, Joe Medwick and Mize.

Although he never played on a pennant-winner with the Cardinals, Mize wound up his career by appearing in five consecutive World Series with the Yankees.

Highlights: The Big Cat played in 10 All-Star Games, four as a Cardinal ... Topped the league in homers four times—twice as a Cardinal, twice as a Giant ... Batted an N.L.-leading .349 for St. Louis in 1939 and hit .364 for the Cards in 1937.

MVP Johnny

POSITION 1st base   **UNIFORM NO** 10   **CARDINALS SEASONS** 1936-41

1981

Highlights: His hallmark season was 1968, when he went 22-9 with 13 shutouts and a 1.12 ERA (the lowest figure in major league history) ... **Five-time 20-game winner** ... Won Cy Young Award in 1968 and 1970 and N.L. MVP honor in '68 ... **Had 28 complete games in '68 and '69.**

Career stats:
251 victories
2.91 ERA
3,117 strikeouts
56 shutouts

GIBSON Bob

POSITION Pitcher   **UNIFORM NO** 45   **CARDINALS SEASONS** 1959-75

Many longtime baseball observers agree that if there was one game they absolutely had to win, the pitcher they would want on the mound is Bob Gibson.

Gibson didn't talk to opponents. He barely talked to his St. Louis teammates on the days he was pitching, and he rarely smiled. Gibson's competitiveness was part of what made him so successful. He once hit a batter in a spring-training game because the player had attempted a bunt. He dusted off former teammates. He glowered.

Gibson was at his fiercest competitive level in the biggest games. In nine career World Series starts, he fashioned a composite 1.89 ERA. In his spectacular 1968 season, a year in which he posted an unfathomable 1.12 ERA and threw 13 shutouts, Gibson had one stretch in which he allowed only two runs in 95 innings. When a line drive off the bat of Roberto Clemente broke his right leg in July 1967, Gibson faced three more batters before falling to the ground. He knew he was hurting, but he didn't know he had suffered a fracture.

It was partly because of Gibson's performance in '68 that baseball officials decided to lower the mound from 15 inches to 10 inches in an effort to inject more offense into the game. The move worked—except, of course, when Gibson was pitching.

1981

Enos SLAUGHTER

POSITION Outfield **UNIFORM NO** 9 **CARDINALS SEASONS** 1938-42, 1946-53

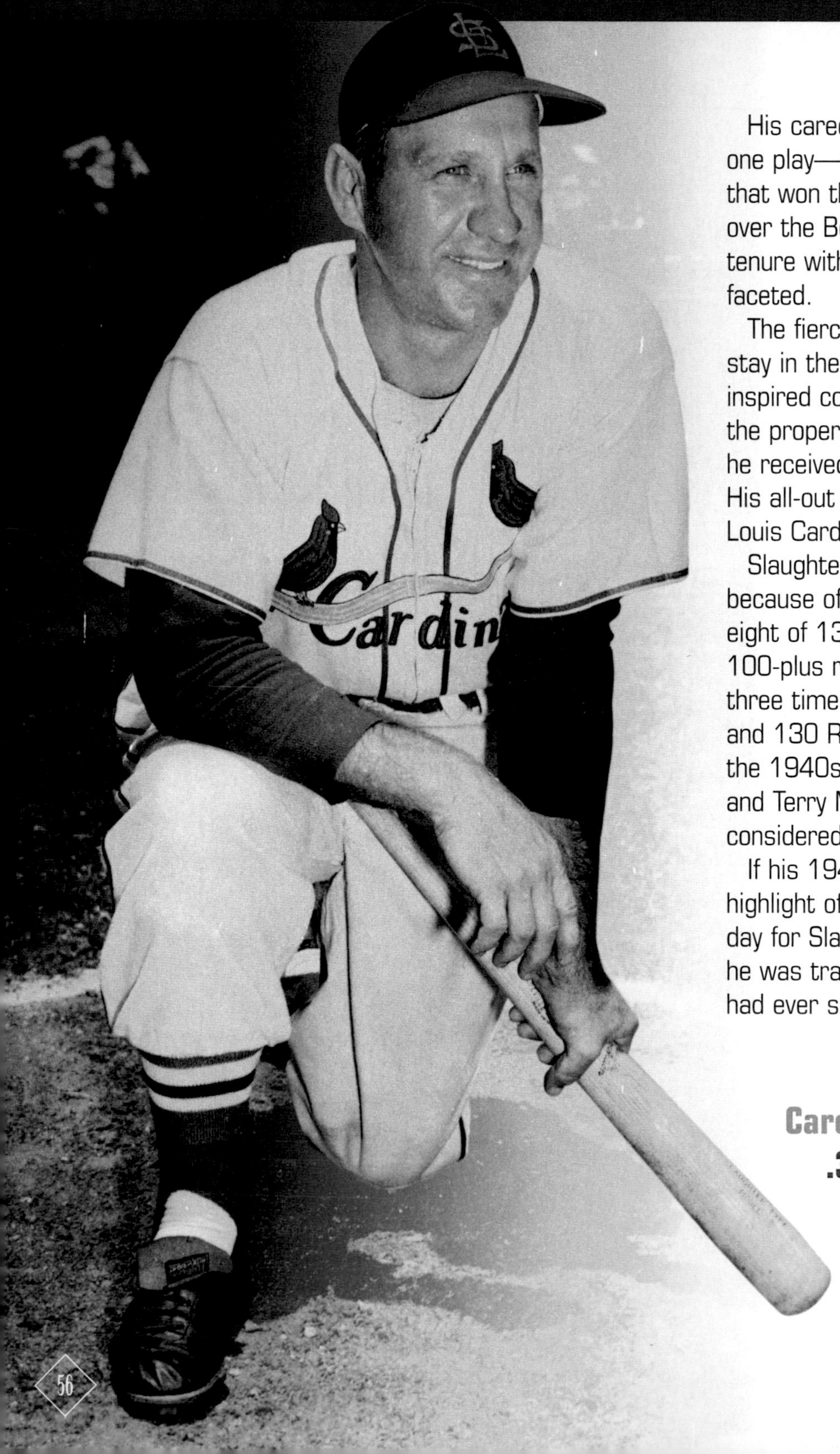

His career is remembered primarily because of one play—the first-to-home "mad dash" in Game 7 that won the 1946 World Series for the Cardinals over the Boston Red Sox. But Enos Slaughter's tenure with the Cardinals was, in fact, multifaceted.

The fiercely competitive Slaughter was a mainstay in the Cardinals' outfield for 13 seasons. He inspired countless youngsters to play the game the proper way—by hustling all of the time, advice he received as a minor leaguer and never forgot. His all-out style made him a quintessential St. Louis Cardinal, and he wore the uniform proudly.

Slaughter, who missed three prime years because of military service, hit .300 or higher in eight of 13 seasons with St. Louis. He drove in 100-plus runs three times and scored 100 runs three times. In 1946, he had 18 home runs and 130 RBIs; in 1949, he batted .336. During the 1940s, when he teamed with Stan Musial and Terry Moore, the Cardinals' outfield was considered one of the greatest of all time.

If his 1946 sprint to home plate was the highlight of his Cardinals career, the darkest day for Slaughter came in April 1954, when he was traded to the Yankees. No injury he had ever suffered hurt quite as much.

Career stats:

.300 batting average

2,383 hits

1,304 RBIs

Highlights: Played in 10 All-Star Games as a Cardinal and hit .381 ... In 1949, he batted .336 with 96 RBIs ... Topped 100-RBI mark three times and had a league-leading 130 RBIs in 1946 ... Had 10 or more triples in a season seven times ... Traded to Yankees in 1954. Played in more World Series as a Yankee (three) than as a Cardinal (two).

To most people, the distance between first base and second base is 90 feet. To Lou Brock, it was 13 steps.

A math major in college, Brock viewed the art of basestealing differently than most. It was no surprise, of course, when Brock set out to steal; whenever he reached first base at Busch Stadium, chants of "Lou, Lou, Lou" echoed throughout the ballpark. He viewed the inner game between himself and the pitcher and catcher as psychological warfare. Everyone knew he was going to go, but only Brock knew when—and exactly how many steps the journey would take.

Much of the reason for Brock's success, both as a hitter and a basestealer, was his attitude. He wasn't afraid to fail—in fact, Brock was driven to be successful, and it was never more apparent starting in June 1964 when St. Louis acquired the outfielder from the Cubs in a trade that some "experts" at the time believed favored the Chicago club. Once he put on a Cardinals uniform, Brock played like a man possessed. He sparked the Cards to the '64 pennant, hitting .348 and stealing 33 bases in 103 games.

The big name who went the other way in the deal, former 20-game winner Ernie Broglio, won only seven games in the rest of his career. Brock, who later had a 118-steal season and finished his career with 938 stolen bases and 3,023 hits, won a lot more—the hearts of every Cardinals fan.

Highlights: Set season (118) and career (938) stolen-base records. Both marks have been shattered by Rickey Henderson ... Helped the Cardinals to the 1967 World Series title with a .414 average, seven stolen bases and eight runs scored ... In the '68 Series, he hit .464 with another seven steals ... His career average in Series play: .391 ... 3,000th hit came off the Cubs' Dennis Lamp on August 13, 1979.

BROCK
Lou

Career stats:
938 stolen bases
3,023 hits
.293 batting average

1985

SCHOENDIENST
Red

Highlights: Led National League second basemen in fielding percentage seven times (four years as a Cardinal), still an N.L. record ... Played in eight All-Star Games as a Cardinal—won 1950 game with a 14th-inning homer at Comiskey Park ... Not a power hitter but had 79-RBI seasons for St. Louis in 1953 and 1954.

Career stats:
.289 batting average
2,449 hits
.982 fielding pct.

60

1989

One of the least-appreciated persons in Cardinals history has to be the driver of the dairy truck who in the early 1940s picked up a red-haired boy in Illinois, a youngster who was hitchhiking to St. Louis to attend a tryout camp.

That boy, Albert "Red" Schoendienst, spent the night sleeping on a park bench outside the St. Louis train station before going out and impressing Cardinals executive Branch Rickey. The kid was signed to a minor league contract.

Rickey marveled at Schoendienst's natural ability, but he didn't know that the prospect would have been even better had it not been for an eye injury. When he was building fences a few years earlier, Schoendienst was struck in the eye by a ricocheting nail. Doctors at first feared they would have to remove the eye, but Schoendienst begged them not to take it, saying he was

going to be a baseball player.

The fact he worked so hard with eye exercises to overcome the injury was a testament to Schoendienst's work ethic, which he learned as young boy.

Red spent two-plus seasons in the minors, then went on to a 19-year major league career that featured 15 seasons with the Cardinals. The ever-dependable second baseman challenged for the National League batting title in 1953, batting .342. Three years earlier, he won the All-Star Game for the N.L. with a 14th-inning home run.

Named Cardinals manager in 1965, Schoendienst expected the same effort from his players that he had put forth. He guided the Cards for 12 seasons (along with two interim assignments), the longest managerial tenure in franchise history. In 1967, he directed St. Louis to the World Series championship.

After listening to Cardinals games for years, a young Harry Caray thought he could do a better job than the broadcasters on hand—so he asked radio station KMOX for a tryout. Caray got the audition, but he didn't get the position. He was terrible.

Caray, who grew up in the St. Louis area, finally earned a chance to do the games on a smaller station. And, after Cardinals owner Sam Breadon decided to have only one station carry the broadcasts in 1947, Caray was hired as the lead broadcaster. He wound up calling Cards game from 1945 through 1969.

The Cardinals had no bigger fan than Caray, and no one did a better job of selling the team. Because of the team's far-flung radio network (which featured smaller stations throughout the Midwest and South), Caray was the main source of information about the club for countless fans. He got emotionally involved on each play, too, saying he wanted his broadcasts to sound as if they were being called by a fan. And that's exactly how Caray's play-by-play came across.

When the Cardinals began their late-season surge for the pennant in 1964, Caray developed a jingle—"the Cardinals are coming, tra la la la." The refrain only increased his popularity, which by any standard was considerable.

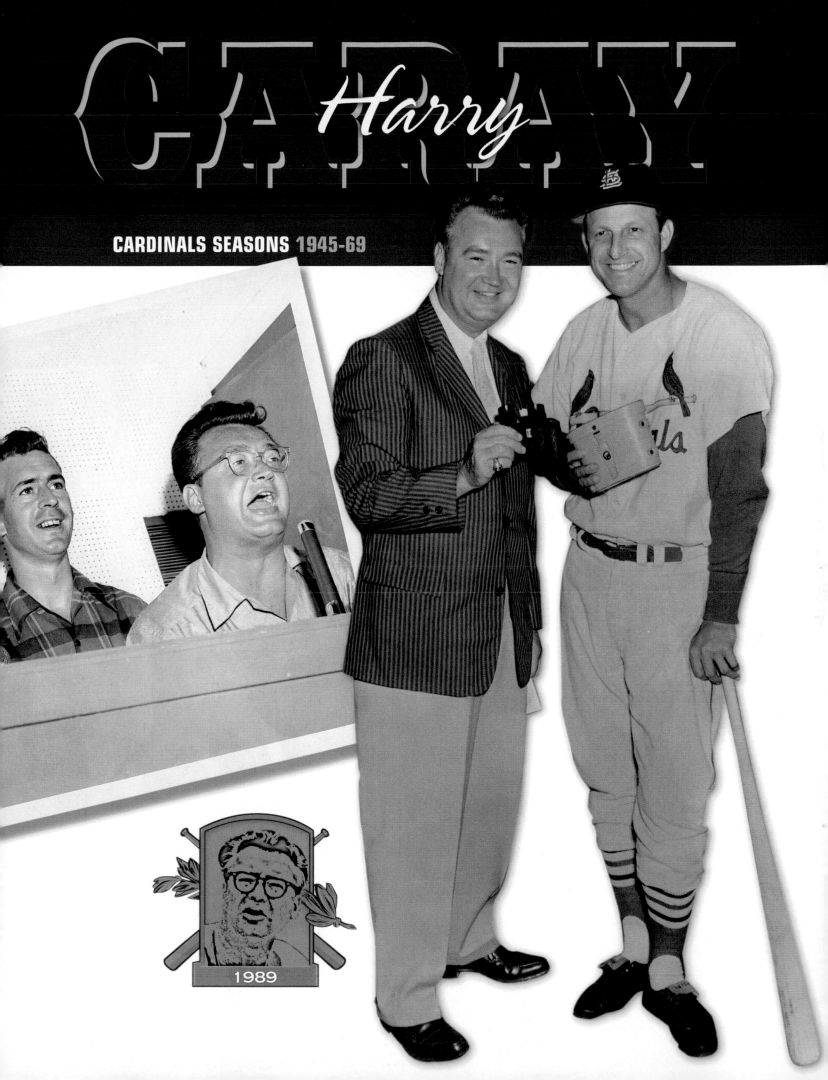

CARAY
Harry

CARDINALS SEASONS 1945-69

1989

BUCK Jack

St. Louis has had more than its share of popular and gifted baseball broadcasters, beginning with France Laux and continuing with Dizzy Dean, Harry Caray and Joe Garagiola. Yet the list will always be topped by Jack Buck.

Buck joined the Cardinals' radio team in 1954, and he served as Caray's sidekick through the 1969 season. He moved into the No. 1 job in 1970 and has remained there.

Cardinals fans' recollections of the team's great moments over the last three decades are always linked to where the fans were and what they were doing when Buck made his memorable calls. Highlights have included Bob Gibson's no-hitter; Lou Brock's record-breaking steals; Bruce Sutter's World Series-ending strikeout; Ozzie Smith and Jack Clark's postseason homers; and Mark McGwire's

1987

pursuit of Roger Maris' home run record.

It has not been unusual for fans to turn down the sound on their television sets so they could watch the game but listen to Buck's broadcast on radio. He has had the ability to entertain, as well as inform, and to do it in his unique style.

Perhaps the biggest secret to his success is that Buck has taken the game—but not himself—seriously. He considers himself fortunate to be a baseball broadcaster, always remembering that the fans, ultimately, are his real bosses.

WORLD SERIES
CHAMPIONS

World Series Champions

A new word was added to baseball's lexicon in 1982—Whiteyball. The definition of the word was provided by the Cardinals themselves, who collectively played with a style and strategy that most people weren't accustomed to seeing. While longtime Orioles manager Earl Weaver, for one, preferred to wait for a three-run homer, Cardinals manager Whitey Herzog and his bunch didn't wait for anything to happen—they made it happen.

The '82 Cardinals ran at every opportunity, and they scooted all the way to the National League pennant and World Series championship. The accomplishment was particularly rewarding for Series first-timer Herzog, whose Kansas City Royals had lost three times in American League Championship Series matchups against the Yankees in the 1970s.

With his team playing in spacious Busch Stadium, Herzog knew the

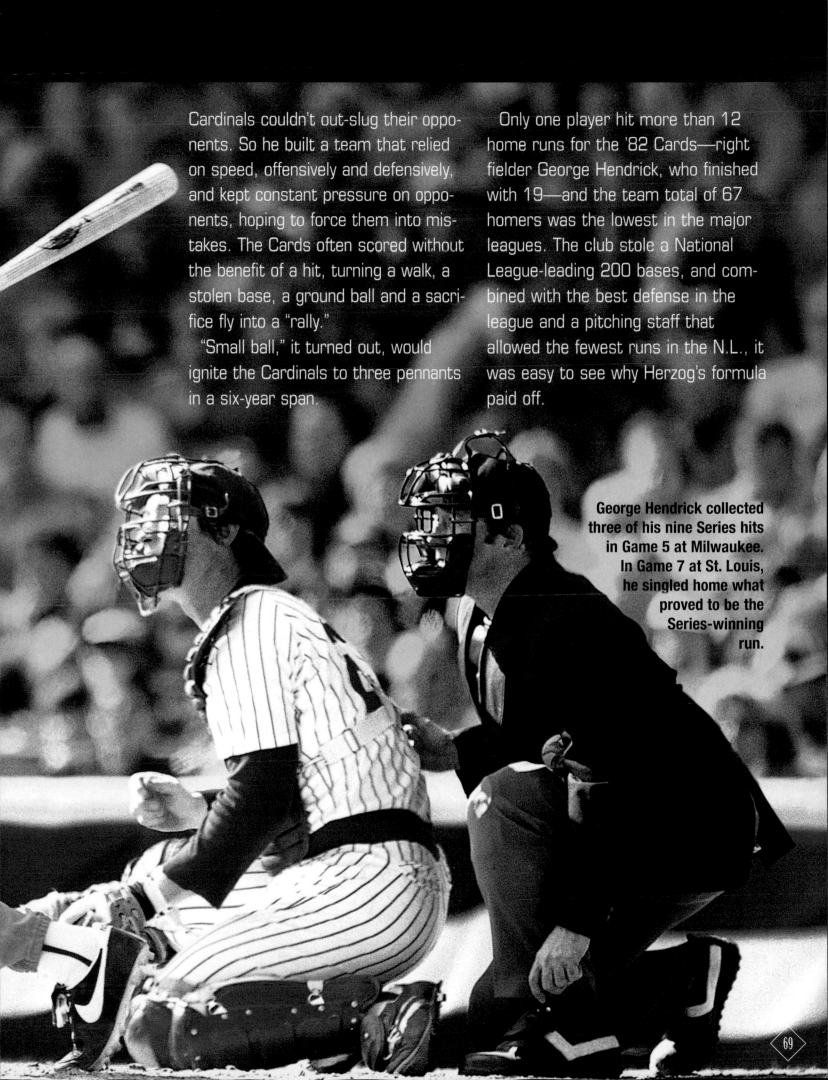

Cardinals couldn't out-slug their opponents. So he built a team that relied on speed, offensively and defensively, and kept constant pressure on opponents, hoping to force them into mistakes. The Cards often scored without the benefit of a hit, turning a walk, a stolen base, a ground ball and a sacrifice fly into a "rally."

"Small ball," it turned out, would ignite the Cardinals to three pennants in a six-year span.

Only one player hit more than 12 home runs for the '82 Cards—right fielder George Hendrick, who finished with 19—and the team total of 67 homers was the lowest in the major leagues. The club stole a National League-leading 200 bases, and combined with the best defense in the league and a pitching staff that allowed the fewest runs in the N.L., it was easy to see why Herzog's formula paid off.

George Hendrick collected three of his nine Series hits in Game 5 at Milwaukee. In Game 7 at St. Louis, he singled home what proved to be the Series-winning run.

69

The infield of Keith Hernandez, Tommy Herr, Ozzie Smith (acquired from San Diego) and Ken Oberkfell combined for only 44 errors. Bob Forsch and Joaquin Andujar led the pitching staff with 15 wins each, and Bruce Sutter was baseball's most dominant closer, saving 36 games. Two rookies, Dave LaPoint and John Stuper, pitched effectively, as did Steve Mura, obtained in another Herzog trade with the Padres.

Some of the off-field moves engineered by Herzog in his dual role as manager and general manager paid huge dividends. Ozzie Smith came over in a trade for fellow shortstop Garry Templeton and immediately flashed the wizardry that would amaze teammates, rivals and fans into the mid-1990s. Lonnie Smith was obtained from the Indians in a three-team deal and became the quality leadoff hitter the Cardinals needed to make their attack work.

The Cardinals also got a little lucky, as happens to

Bruce Sutter got the glad hand from manager Whitey Herzog after saving Game 3. Bob Forsch (right) was the Cards' starter and loser in Game 1 in St. Louis and also dropped Game 5 in Milwaukee. Ozzie Smith (left, sliding) scored three runs, had five hits and played errorless ball in his first World Series.

most good teams. When center fielder David Green was sidelined with a hamstring injury in May, St. Louis summoned an unknown player from the minor leagues and told him he likely would be in the majors for just a few weeks—until Green was healthy again. The call-up, Willie McGee, wound up staying for nearly a decade (and later returned to the club), becoming one of the franchise's most popular and successful players.

A 12-game winning streak in April convinced the Cardinals they were good enough to win, and the stable starting pitching and the presence of Sutter in the bullpen kept the team from a prolonged losing streak. In fact, the Cards never lost more than three consecutive games until the last week of the season—after they had wrapped up the East Division title.

If the Cardinals had any doubts that 1982 was going to be their year, they were erased on a Sunday afternoon in August when third-string catcher Glenn Brummer—not exactly one of the team's speedsters—stole home with two out in the 12th inning of a game against the Giants at Busch.

Most St. Louis fans still remember where they were when Brummer made his startling game-winning steal—just like they recall what they were doing when Smith and Jack Clark hit dramatic playoff homers three years later.

Joaquin Andujar won Game 3 for the Cards but was felled by a seventh-inning line drive.

"A guy told me he was listening on the radio and drove off the highway," Brummer said. "Another guy told me he was barbecuing and knocked his grill over. I guess it shocked them so much they haven't forgotten."

Thus inspired, the Cardinals went on to clinch the division title and prepared for their first postseason berth in 14 years. Their opponent in the N.L. Championship Series was not determined until the last day of the regular season, when Atlanta clinched the West Division crown—thanks to a final-game loss by the second-place Dodgers.

Ken Oberkfell and the Cardinals were upended by Robin Yount (sliding) and the Brewers, 10-0, in Game 1. St. Louis rebounded, thanks in part to the solid play of rookie Willie McGee (right), who scored six runs in the Series, had five RBIs and played great defense.

The Cardinals were losing the NLCS opener to the Braves' Phil Niekro, 1-0, when rain halted the game two outs before it would have become official. After a long delay, the

game was postponed. Whether that was divine intervention or not, the Cards went on to sweep the Braves and advanced to the World Series against the Milwaukee Brewers.

It was fitting, perhaps, that the Cardinals and Brewers emerged to play in the Series since Herzog, in his G.M. days, had conduct-ed some major business with Milwaukee. He had traded Rollie Fingers and longtime Cardinals favorite Ted Simmons, among others, to the Brewers. Herzog, who gave up his front-office role in April 1982, joked that he should have been named "general manager of the year"—in Milwaukee.

No one in St. Louis was laughing after Game 1 of the World Series, a 10-0 romp for the Brewers, but the Cardinals rebounded. Getting spectacular all-around play from McGee, key hitting from catcher Darrell Porter and Hernandez and standout pitching from Joaquin Andujar, Stuper and Sutter, St. Louis forced a seventh game. The Cards won the finale, 6-3, thanks to a three-run rally in the sixth inning capped by Hendrick's go-ahead single. Sutter provided St. Louis with one of its greatest baseball moments when he struck out Gorman Thomas to end the Series.

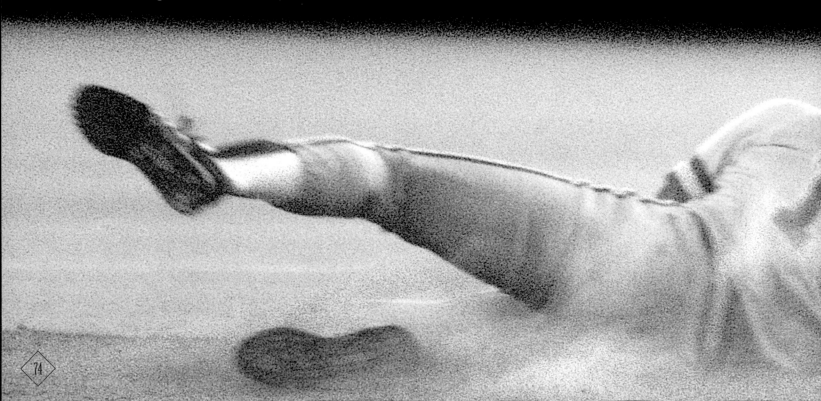

Smith, playing his first season with the Cardinals, exhibited his acrobatic style time and again in the 1982 Series. He took part in five double plays and handled all 39 of his chances flawlessly. Sutter (opposite page) demonstrated his skills, too, posting one victory and two saves. Sutter ended the Series with a strikeout of Brewers slugger Gorman Thomas.

It was celebration time after Game 7. Commissioner Bowie Kuhn, with broadcaster Bob Costas holding forth, presented the championship trophy to owner Gussie Busch and manager Whitey Herzog. Meanwhile, Jim Kaat poured some bubbly on Dave LaPoint's head. Cardinals standouts Keith Hernandez and Lonnie Smith (lower left) had exchanged high-fives earlier.

Herzog was happy for all of his players, but especially for those he had worked so hard to bring to St. Louis, like Porter, who had been with him in

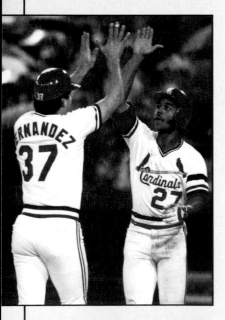

Kansas City and had fought back from alcohol and drug abuse. Porter was named the MVP of both the NLCS and World Series.

He also was happy for team owner Gussie Busch, who had given Herzog the freedom he needed to build the team and had been rewarded with another championship.

Herzog and the Cardinals thought they had been cheated out of the division title a year earlier in a strike-interrupted season. Even though they had the best overall record in the division, they didn't win either half of the split season and thereby didn't qualify for the playoffs. Winning the 1982 World Series eased the frustration—mightily.

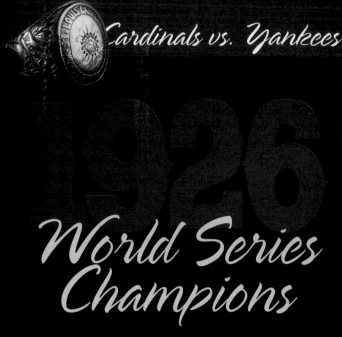

1926
World Series Champions

Talk about having to win the pennant the hard way. After the Cardinals defeated the Pirates on September 1, 1926, they held a one-game lead over the Reds in the National League race. They also had just completed their home schedule.

Because of a scheduling quirk, the Cardinals had to play their final 24 regular-season games on the road—with a visit to each of their seven league rivals. The schedule certainly not in their favor, the Cards nevertheless played well enough on the road—they went 13-11—to claim the first pennant in franchise history. St. Louis finished two games ahead of Cincinnati.

The results might have been different if not for two front-office moves. On June 14, general manager Branch Rickey obtained outfielder Billy Southworth in a trade with the Giants. Southworth became the Cardinals' regular right fielder—and a solid contributor.

On June 22, Cardinals owner Sam Breadon saw that the Cubs had placed veteran pitcher Grover Cleveland Alexander on waivers. With Rickey out of town on a scouting trip, Breadon contacted manager Rogers Hornsby to get his opinion on Alexander. Hornsby's reaction: Claim him.

Alexander turned out to be a great addition to the club—

Babe Ruth stole second base on this play in Game 6—and he took down Cards shortstop Tommy Thevenow in the process. With two out in the ninth inning of Game 7 and St. Louis ahead, 3-2, Ruth attempted another steal and was nailed on catcher Bob O'Farrell's throw to second baseman Rogers Hornsby.

even before he struck out the Yankees' Tony Lazzeri to preserve the Cardinals' lead in the seventh inning of Game 7 of the World Series.

Because the Cardinals had never played in a World Series, St. Louisans didn't know exactly how to respond when the team came back to St. Louis after splitting the first two games of the Series with the Yankees in New York. But respond they did.

The *St. Louis Globe-Democrat* devoted its front page to

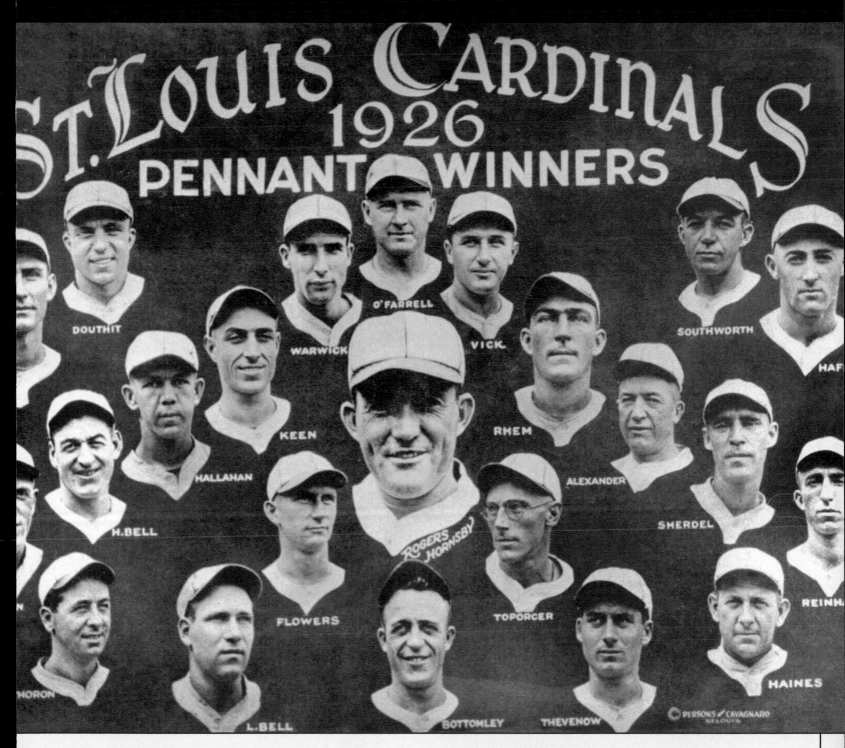

ST.LOUIS CARDINALS
1926
PENNANT WINNERS

DOUTHIT   WARWICK   O'FARRELL   VICK.   SOUTHWORTH   HAF

KEEN   RHEM

HALLAHAN   ALEXANDER

H.BELL   ROGERS HORNSBY   SHERDEL

FLOWERS   TOPORCER   REINH

HORON   L.BELL   BOTTOMLEY   THEVENOW   HAINES

© PERSONS & CAVAGNARO
ST.LOUIS

Game 3, punctuating its coverage with a banner headline that screamed: "GREATEST DEMONSTRA-TION IN CITY'S BASEBALL HISTORY STAGED AS FRENZIED MULTITUDES LIONIZE BASEBALL HEROES AMID BEDLAM OF NOISE AND JOYOUS ENTHUSIASM."

The Cardinals' triumph in Game 7 at Yankee Stadium touched off another major celebration that didn't end until long after the team's victory train had pulled back into Union Station from New York.

Of course, Southworth and Alexander weren't the only standouts on the '26 Cardinals. Besides Alexander, there were four other future Hall of Famers on the club—Hornsby, Jim Bottomley, Chick Hafey and Jesse Haines. Catcher Bob O'Farrell was the league's Most Valuable Player; Bottomley led the N.L. in RBIs and total bases; and pitcher Flint Rhem tied for the most wins in the N.L.

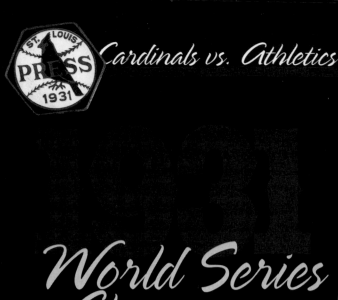

World Series Champions

The 1931 season saw the emergence of a player who would turn out to be the sparkplug for the decade's great Gas House Gang teams: a 27-year-old outfielder named Pepper Martin, who previously had managed only 14 at-bats in the major leagues.

John Leonard Martin got his nickname in the minor leagues, and it stuck because it reflected his style on the field. He knew only one way to play—all out, all the time.

Martin's uniform was always dirty.

The Oklahoma native took over the starting spot in center field in June—after the Cardinals dealt Taylor Douthit to Cincinnati—and St. Louis never looked back, easily winning its second consecutive pennant.

The Cardinals reached the 100-victory plateau for the first time in franchise history and became the first National League team to top the century mark in 18 years. They finished 13 games ahead of the second-place Giants.

Martin's play was inspiring to even older Cardinals players, like Frankie Frisch, who was named the league's MVP. Frisch led the Cardinals in only one major offensive statistical category, stolen bases (28, a league-leading total), but he was recognized for his steady play and leadership on a team that featured five future Hall of Famers.

As good as the regular lineup was—and the presence of Frisch, Chick Hafey, Jim Bottomley and Martin made it mighty good—the Cardinals were particularly dangerous because of deep starting pitching, led by lefthander Bill Hallahan, rookie Paul Derringer and veteran spitballer Burleigh Grimes. Hallahan tied for the league lead in wins, and the trio combined for 54 victories. Three other pitchers also

The Cardinals' Pepper Martin carried a big stick in the 1931 Series, collecting 12 hits against the A's. As reflected by his nickname, Martin was known for his all-out play.

were double-figure winners.

Martin, who from 1924 through 1930 spent most of his playing time in the minors, brought excitement to the team. He was always a prankster, once registering in a hotel as gangster Pretty Boy Floyd. The local sheriff wasn't amused.

Martin, who made one pinch-running appearance in the 1928 World Series after playing sparingly for the Cardinals in the regular season, was determined not to sit idly by in the 1931 Fall Classic. He didn't, either. Martin collected 12 hits, drove in five runs and stole five bases as the Cardinals upset the Philadelphia Athletics to win their second Series championship.

When commissioner Kenesaw Mountain Landis visited the Cardinals' clubhouse to offer his congratulations, he told Martin, "I'd rather trade places with you than any other man in the country."

Replied Martin: "That will be fine, Judge—if we can trade salaries, too."

Veteran Burleigh Grimes won 17 regular-season games in 1931 and Frankie Frisch (inset) was named the N.L.'s MVP. Grimes won twice in the World Series, taking Games 3 and 7.

World Series Champions

Joe Medwick's hard slide into third baseman Marv Owen in Game 7 angered Detroit fans, who threw debris onto the field. Commissioner Kenesaw Mountain Landis met with manager Frankie Frisch (3) and Medwick, and he ordered Medwick out of the game.

After Frankie Frisch took over as Cardinals manager during the 1933 season, he was determined to mold the team in his style. Not only did he want players who were aggressive, but he wanted players who exhibited discipline and gave 100 percent effort at all times.

Starting in spring training in 1934, Frisch established strict rules that he wanted his players to follow—no drinking or gambling and a midnight curfew for players on the road. He wasn't dealing with a bunch of choir boys, either—not with such players as Pepper Martin and Dizzy Dean on the roster.

Dean wasn't about to let a new set of rules change his behavior. He was joined in some of his escapades in the summer of '34 by brother Paul, a rookie who proved to be a major addition to the rotation.

Upset about the prospect of taking a trip to Detroit to play an exhibition game in the middle of the pennant race, the

Having the Tigers by the tail was a happy experience for the Cardinals' Dizzy Dean, who found time to joke with humorist Will Rogers after breezing to a six-hit, 11-0 victory over Detroit in Game 7. St. Louis played without left fielder Medwick from the middle of the sixth inning on, but by that time Dean and the National League champs had a 9-0 lead.

Dean brothers intentionally missed the train. Frisch announced he was fining and suspending both players. That made the Deans even more irate, and it looked as if the brouhaha might upend the Cardinals' pennant hopes.

Dizzy even tore up two uniforms to show reporters and photographers his displeasure. After about a week, the entire dispute was settled—Paul was reinstated first, then Diz. It was just in time for the brothers to lead the Cardinals' charge to the pennant.

Dizzy became a 30-game winner by winning four times in the sea-son's final 10 days. Paul threw a no-hitter on September 21 and posted 19 victories overall, enabling the duo to surpass Dizzy's spring-training prediction that the brothers would combine for 45 wins.

The surging Cardinals overcame a 5½-game deficit to the Giants with 17 games to play. The Cards clinched the pennant on the final day of the season, an afternoon on which Dizzy racked up win No. 30 by shutting out the Reds. Dean was named the league's MVP.

Waiting to play the Cardinals in the World Series were the Detroit Tigers, and Dean again was able to back up his prediction of a Cardinals victory—although Detroit did not go down meekly.

The Series went to Game 7, which forever will be remembered because of Joe Medwick's removal from the game after his hard slide into third base riled the Detroit crowd. With fans hurling bottles, fruit and vegetables onto the field in the sixth inning, commissioner Kenesaw Mountain Landis ordered Medwick out of the game. No matter. The Gas House Gang, with Dizzy Dean in full control, was en route to an 11-0 victory.

World Series Champions

Manager Billy Southworth was outnumbered by Yankees and umpires in a 1942 Series dispute—but the scoreboard favored his Cardinals, who won in five games.

With the Cardinals trailing the Brooklyn Dodgers by 9½ games on the morning of August 16, general manager Branch Rickey probably had a lot of people agreeing with him when he lamented, "We don't have a chance."

Luckily for Rickey and the Cardinals, none of the people agreeing with him were St. Louis players.

Putting on one of the most incredible finishes in baseball history, manager Billy Southworth's 1942 Cardinals won 41 of their final 48 games and stormed to the National League pennant.

The Cards forged a first-place tie less than a month after facing that 9½-game deficit, then moved into first place—to stay—on September 13 when they split a doubleheader against the Phillies and the Dodgers lost two games to the Reds. St. Louis clinched the pennant on the final day of the season, completing a 20-4 September run. Brooklyn was 16-10 in the last month.

The Cardinals' 106 victories set a franchise record that still stands. There were myriad reasons for the team's success, starting with the pitching. The staff ERA of 2.55 was the lowest in the majors since 1919. Mort Cooper won 22 games, fashioned a 1.78 ERA and threw 10 shutouts. He was named the National League's MVP. Rookie Johnny Beazley went 21-6. Cooper, who wore uniform No. 13, was stuck on 13 victories in 1942, so he switched to No. 14 and promptly got his 14th win. He then wore No. 15 and posted his 15th triumph, and on it went—all the way to 22.

The team's offense, while not posting overwhelming numbers, was solid. Stan Musial, playing his first full major league season, was the left fielder and batted .315. Gifted center fielder Terry Moore hit .288, and right fielder Enos Slaughter led the team with a .318 mark and also contributed team-high totals of 13 home runs and 98 RBIs.

The left side of the infield, manned by standout shortstop Marty Marion and rookie Whitey Kurowski, was first-rate.

It was the youth of the team that prompted most observers to pick the Yankees to win the World Series. But Musial and company weren't awed by the New Yorkers and went out and proved it, winning the Fall Classic in five games. Kurowski provided the big moment, breaking a 2-2 tie in Game 5 with a Series-deciding two-run homer in the ninth inning.

After the clincher, winning pitcher Johnny Beazley (with glove) and batting star Whitey Kurowski (next to Beazley, facing camera) celebrated the Cards' title with Southworth and Harry Walker (both sitting), Enos Slaughter and Stan Musial.

DORRILL PHOTO

ST. LOUIS CARDINALS...1942

From the left, back row...FRANK CRESPI, COAKER TRIPLETT, ERVIN DUSAK, RAY SANDERS, TERRY MOORE, MAX LANIE, MORTON COOPER, HOWARD KRIST, MURRY DICKSON, LLOYD MOORE and BUTCH YATKEMAN, club-house attendant. Center row...DR. H. J. WEAVER, trainer; BILL BECKMANN, JIM BROWN, HARRY WALKER, JOHN BEAZLEY, ERNIE WHITE, ENOS SLAUGHTER, HARRY GUMBERT, HOWARD POLLET, WALKER COOPER, JOFF CROSS and LEO WARD, Secy. Front row...MARTY MARION, STAN MUSIAL, JOHNNY HOPP, Coach MIKE GONZALES, Manager BILLY SOUTHWORTH, Coach BUZZY WARES, GEORGE KUROWSKI, SAM NARRON and KEN O'DEA.

World Series Champions

The Browns' Al Zarilla raced across first base in the fourth inning of Game 5 after hitting a ground ball to Cardinals pitcher Mort Cooper. Ray Sanders (5) already had taken Cooper's throw for the putout, and he quickly stepped off the bag.

The Cardinals had won previous championships in almost every way possible—in a tight race, via a runaway, with outstanding hitting and because of overwhelming pitching. The story of the 1944 Cardinals was highlighted by a record-setting defense.

Led by shortstop Marty Marion, who had taken over as the team's veteran leader in the absence of Terry Moore, the Cardinals set a major league record with a .982 fielding percentage. Four St. Louis players led the National League in fielding at their positions—Marion, first baseman Ray Sanders, third baseman Whitey Kurowski and center fielder Johnny Hopp. Marion was named the league's Most Valuable Player, despite hitting only .267 with 63 runs batted in. Six players on his own team hit more home runs, six hit for a higher average and six drove in more runs, but to a man the Cards agreed Marion was the MVP.

Sanders drove in 102 runs, Hopp batted .336 and fast-emerging outfielder Stan Musial hit .347.

Another secret to the Cardinals' success was their ability to adequately replace all of their stars who had left for military service. Harry Walker, Lou Klein, Al Brazle, Howie Krist and Ernie White departed for duty before the season began, and Red Munger joined them in the middle of the year. Moore, Enos Slaughter and Johnny Beazley had left after the 1942 season.

Mort Cooper was a 22-game winner, Ted Wilks and Max Lanier each had 17 victories and Harry Brecheen won 16 games as the Cardinals finished with 105 wins for the second consecutive season. They had won 106 in 1942.

The Cardinals turned the pennant race into a rout in July, and they opened a 20-game lead by the end of August. Only a September slump—they lost 15 of 20 games in one stretch—kept them from challenging the league record of 116 wins.

The Cardinals' Sanders scored a fourth-inning run in Game 2, sliding across the plate after Emil Verban's fly ball to left field. The Browns' catcher was Red Hayworth. Sanders scored the game-deciding run on an 11th-inning pinch single by Ken O'Dea. The A.L. champions had won Game 1 the day before and happily milled about the dugout (below).

The only suspense for the Cardinals was whom they would face in the World Series, and it turned out to be the St. Louis Browns, with whom they shared Sportsman's Park. The Browns would be making the only World Series appearance in franchise history.

Most baseball people thought post-season experience gave manager Billy Southworth and the Cardinals an advantage. The Browns proved tougher than expected in the Streetcar Series, though, winning two of the first three games. But starters Brecheen, Cooper and Lanier and reliever Wilks held the American Leaguers to two runs in the next three games—the N.L. champions won, 5-1, 2-0 and 3-1—and the Cardinals were World Series champions for the second time in three seasons.

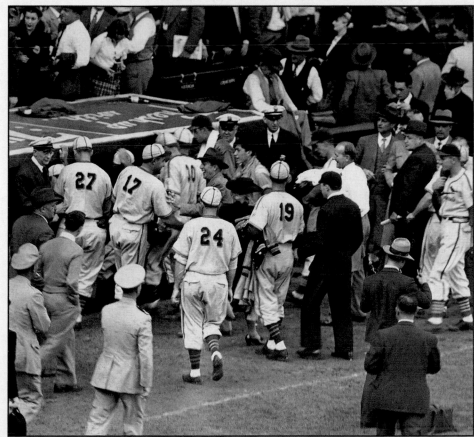

World Series Champions

With their stars returning from military service, the Cardinals began the 1946 season with great expectations. Their fans were thinking the same way, and they turned out in record numbers. For the first time in franchise history, home attendance reached one million.

What no one knew was the obstacles that would have to be overcome for St. Louis to win its fourth pennant in five years. Pitchers Johnny Beazley and Ernie White returned from military service with arm injuries. In late May, the Mexican League raided the Cardinals, signing pitchers Max Lanier and Fred Martin and second baseman Lou Klein. And Red Barrett, who had won 21 games for the Cards in 1945, was ineffective.

Yet St. Louis persevered.

Klein's departure opened an infield spot for Red Schoendienst, who as a rookie in 1945 had played left field. Schoendienst became a fixture at second base. Stan Musial, who previously had been used exclusively in the outfield, saw extensive duty at first base in his return to the club after one year in the Navy. The year away didn't hurt Musial. He won the league's MVP award after leading the National League in almost every major offensive category.

Enos Slaughter won the league's RBI crown, and Whitey Kurowski batted .301.

As was the case for much of th[e]

Johnny Pesky made life difficult for Red Schoendienst in the sixth inning of Game 6, but the Cardinals' second baseman was able to complete a double play.

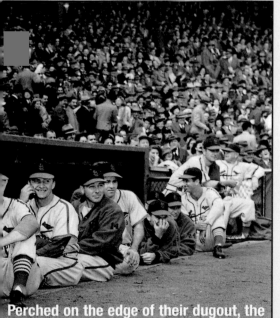

Perched on the edge of their dugout, the Cards were a confident bunch. They tied a Series mark (since broken) with 20 hits in Game 4, with Terry Moore (above, left) getting the record-equaling hit.

decade, the Cardinals battled Brooklyn for the pennant. On July 2, the Dodgers led by 7½ games; by July 18, the Cards had slipped into the lead, and it was nip and tuck the rest of the way.

Time and again, the teams were tied for first place, and that was the scenario on the final afternoon of the regular season. Former Cardinal Mort Cooper gave his old team a chance to win the pennant that day when, pitching for the Braves, he shut out the Dodgers. But the Cubs defeated manager Eddie Dyer's Cardinals, leaving Brooklyn and St. Louis tied with 96-58 records and forcing the first pennant play-off in major league history.

The format was a best-of-three series, and when the Dodgers won the coin flip, Brooklyn manager Leo Durocher asked that the first game be played in St. Louis, with the second and third game (if necessary) scheduled for Ebbets Field.

There was no third game. The Cardinals won, 4-2 and 8-4, and advanced to the World Series against the Red Sox, who had won their pennant race by 12 games. Harry Brecheen tossed a shutout in Game 2, allowed only one run in Game 6 and won in relief of Murry Dickson in Game 7 after Enos Slaughter's mad dash from first base on Harry Walker's eighth-inning hit provided the winning margin in a 4-3 victory.

1964
World Series Champions

On the night of September 28, the Cardinals had five games to play in the 1964 season. St. Louis had climbed back into the National League pennant race—the club had been 6½ games behind the then-league-leading Phillies eight days earlier—but still was one game out of first place, now held by Cincinnati. Manager Johnny Keane didn't know what the outcome of the race would be, but he did know at least part of his own future.

Writing a letter in longhand, with his wife typing it on a borrowed typewriter, Keane crafted his resignation as manager of the Cardinals. He tucked the letter in his pocket, ready to deliver it to owner August A. Busch Jr. as soon as the Cardinals' season ended.

Little did Keane know the season would last another 2½ weeks, until the Cardinals defeated the Yankees in Game 7 of the World Series. The result didn't change Keane's mind, however, and he announced his resignation the day after the Series ended. Keane had been upset with reports earlier in the season that Busch was preparing to fire him and hire Leo Durocher as manager, and he also was unhappy with the mid-August firing of general manager Bing Devine.

Keane's resignation was almost as shocking as the Cardinals' come-from-behind spurt to win the pennant. Only the true believers among Cardinals fans thought the team could pull it out. But an eight-game winning streak by St. Louis, 10 consecutive losses by the Phillies and four Cincinnati defeats in the Reds' last five games put the Cardinals in position to win the pennant on the final day of the season.

The turning point in the World Series came in the sixth inning of Game 4. The Yankees led the Series, two games to one, and were ahead, 3-0, in this game. Another win and the Yankees would have a commanding lead in the Series. After the Cardinals loaded the bases against Al Downing, team captain Ken Boyer pulled St. Louis ahead by hammering a pitch into the left-field seats. With Roger Craig and Ron Taylor contributing 8⅔ innings of two-hit, scoreless relief, the Cards won the game and evened the Series.

Boyer, the National League's MVP that season, later called

Umpire Bill McKinley ruled that the Yankees' Joe Pepitone, checking his swing, was hit by this Bob Gibson pitch in the sixth inning of Game 2. Cards manager Johnny Keane and players Dick Groat and Tim McCarver (opposite page) argued the ball hit Pepitone's bat.

St. Louis' McCarver (left, sliding past Yankees catcher Elston Howard) showed he could run the bases—and that he was capable of breaking into a home run trot, too. He won Game 5 with a three-run shot in the 10th inning and found a welcoming committee at home plate.

the grand slam the highlight of his career. As he rounded third base, he passed younger brother Clete, playing third base for the Yankees. It was all Clete could do to keep himself from smiling.

After the teams split the next two games—Tim McCarver's three-run homer in the 10th won Game 5—the Cardinals turned to Bob Gibson for Game 7, and he carried a 6-0 lead into the sixth before hanging on for a 7-5 victory. He struck out nine Yankees in a game that gave the Cards their first World Series crown since 1946.

World Series Champions

The acquisition of outfielder Roger Maris from the Yankees proved to be the final piece to the Cardinals' puzzle for 1967. Now strong at all positions, they marched to the National League pennant, moving into first place to stay in June and eventually winning by 10½ games over the Giants.

The addition of Maris allowed Mike Shannon to move from right field to third base, solidifying the lineup and adding winning experience to a team already primed for a big season.

First baseman Orlando Cepeda, obtained from the Giants a year earlier, batted .325 with 25 home runs and 111 RBIs and won the league's Most Valuable Player award. Also powering El Birdos' offense were outfielders Lou Brock and Curt Flood and catcher Tim McCarver.

The pitching staff proved to be just as effective, despite losing Bob Gibson for nearly two months because of a broken leg, suffered when he was hit by a line drive off the bat of the Pirates' Roberto Clemente.

Dick Hughes, a 29-year-old rookie, came out of nowhere and won 16 games, and young Nellie Briles took Gibson's spot in the rotation and won his last nine decisions. Another promising pitcher, lefthander Steve Carlton, won five games while Gibson was out and finished 14-9. The trio of Hughes, Briles and Carlton combined for 44 victories, easing the absence of Gibson.

When Gibson was hurt on July 15, the Cardinals were nursing a four-game lead and many thought their season would unravel. But the steady hand of manager Red Schoendienst helped make certain that didn't happen. In

fact, when Gibson returned to the mound on September 7, the Cardinals' lead had grown to 11½ games. Without their ace, the Cards had gone 36-20.

The easy pennant run didn't leave the Cardinals overconfident for the World Series against the Red Sox, who featured a Triple Crown winner in outfielder Carl Yastrzemski and an ace pitcher of their own in Jim Lonborg.

The Red Sox's 1967 regular season had been called the "The Impossible Dream"—Boston had finished in ninth place in 1966— but the phrase took on another meaning in the World Series. Gibson (three complete-game victories and a home run in Game 7), Brock (.414 average and seven stolen bases), Maris (.385) and the rest of the Cardinals made sure that Boston's dream of winning the Series was just that—impossible.

Bob Gibson (top, left photo), Orlando Cepeda (30) and their teammates had that championship feeling. Gibson went 3-0 in the Series with a 1.00 ERA. Lou Brock (left) scored eight runs and stole seven bases.

1928, 1930, 1943, 1968 1985, 1987 *World Series*

Close. Very close.
 Six times the Cardinals have won the National League pennant but failed to win the World Series. On two of those occasions, a different outcome on one play might have changed the Series outcome. Another time, victory also seemed within the Cards' grasp.

 In 1968, the Cardinals and Detroit Tigers went to Game 7 of the World Series, Bob Gibson matched against Mickey Lolich. The game was scoreless until the seventh inning, when the Tigers put two runners on with two out. Jim Northrup then hit a smash to center field, a drive that Curt Flood normally would have caught easily. This time, he misjudged the ball—he broke in and the ball sailed past him—and it went for a triple. Northrup scored on Bill Freehan's double, and the Tigers parlayed the 3-0 lead into a 4-1 victory.

Bob Gibson dazzled in the 1968 World Series, but the Cardinals blew a three games-to-one lead. A misjudged ball in Game 7 was disastrous.

 In 1985, the telling moment came in Game 6 of the Series against the Kansas City Royals. With the Cardinals one win from the championship, the game was scoreless until the eighth inning, when pinch hitter Brian Harper's RBI single gave St. Louis the lead. That edge held until the bottom of the ninth, when a missed call by first-base umpire Don Denkinger—pinch hitter Jorge Orta was ruled safe on an inning-opening grounder on which replays clearly showed he was out—helped the Royals rally for a 2-1 victory. The winning runs scored on a one-out single by former Cardinal Dane Iorg.

 Inspired, the Royals blasted the Cardinals, 11-0, in Game 7 to capture the Series.

 Two years later, in 1987, the Cardinals found them-

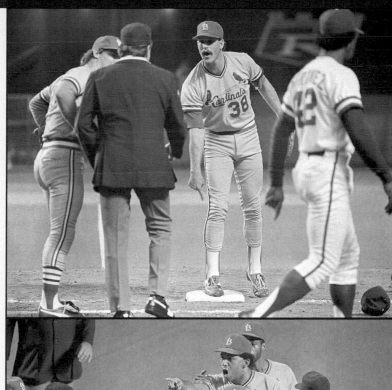

Todd Worrell (38) disputed Don Denkinger's call in Game 6 of the '85 Series. In Game 7, Joaquin Andujar (above, pointing) was ejected. Below are Whitey Herzog, Terry Pendleton, Ozzie Smith, Tommy Herr and Jack Clark.

selves in the same position—with a chance to win the Series in Game 6, this time against the Minnesota Twins. St. Louis was leading, 5-2, in that game, but Gary Gaetti's double and Don Baylor's two-run homer in the fifth inning tied the score and, after the Twins slipped ahead later in that inning, Kent Hrbek followed with a grand slam off Ken Dayley in the sixth. The Twins won, 11-5.

Unlike 1985, Game 7 wasn't a blowout, but the Twins prevailed, 4-2, and became the first team in history to take the World Series by winning all four games at home and none on the road.

The Cardinals' other three World Series losses were painful, but not in such an agonizing "what if" way. The Cards were swept by the Yankees in 1928, lost in six games to the Philadelphia A's in 1930 and fell in five games to the Yankees in 1943.

Three times the Cardinals have advanced to the National League playoffs but lost in the their bid for the pennant. St. Louis was defeated in seven games by the Atlanta Braves in the 1996 N.L. Championship Series (after the Cards had taken a 3-2 lead), lost in five games to the Mets in the 2000 NLCS and came up short in decisive Game 5 of the 2001 Division Series against the Arizona Diamondbacks.

Jim Bottomley (left) and the Cardinals were swept by Babe Ruth and the Yankees in the 1928 World Series. Stan Musial (opposite page, bottom) and company fell to Charlie Keller and the Yanks in the 1943 Series, a five-game Fall Classic in which Marty Marion homered in Game 2 (below) and was met at home plate by Mort Cooper (13). Manager Gabby Street (far right, top) saw his 1930 Cards lose to Connie Mack and the Athletics in a six-game Series in which St. Louis' Charley Gelbert (immediate right, top) and Chick Hafey (sliding) scored runs in Game 4.

The STARTING LINEUP

WHITEY HERZOG

he Whitey Herzog era in St. Louis was best described by the term "Whiteyball," which before long was synonymous with a style of play that emphasized a running game, a wherewithal to manufacture runs and a reliance on a strong defense. Herzog's teams won three pennants (1982, 1985 and 1987) and one World Series ('82), and his 1981 club compiled the best overall record in the N.L. East, only to miss postseason play in the strike-interrupted year when the Cardinals failed to win either half of the makeshift split season. The Cards' exciting brand of ball under the master strategist—and the team's considerable success—resonated with St. Louis fans, who broke the franchise's three-million attendance barrier for the first time in 1987 and topped the figure again two years later.

STAN THE

FIRST BASE

STAN
MUSIAL

MAN

Any list of great players in Cardinals history begins with Stan Musial, a career .331 hitter whose 3,630 hits (1,815 at home, 1,815 on the road) rank fourth in major league history. He is the franchise's all-time leader in games played, hits, home runs, doubles, triples, RBIs, total bases, at-bats, runs and walks. He won three MVP awards and seven N.L. batting titles. He is second in games played by a Cardinals outfielder and third in games played by a Cards first baseman.

ROGERS HORNSBY

No player in franchise history can match the hitting exploits of Rogers Hornsby, who batted .359 in 1,580 games as a Cardinal. Hornsby won six consecutive batting titles while playing for the Cards, three of those crowns coming when he hit .401, .424 and .403 in a four-year span. He later won a seventh batting championship as a member of the Boston Braves. His season hits totals as a Cardinals player included such figures as 250, 235 and 227. Anything but a singles hitter, he led the National League in doubles four times and in home runs twice. Hornsby and Ted Williams are the major leagues' only two-time Triple Crown winners—Hornsby was the National League's batting average/RBI/homer king in 1922 and 1925. Hornsby was player/manager for St. Louis' first World Series champions, the 1926 Cardinals.

THIRD BASE

KEN BOYER

Captain of the Cardinals in the early 1960s, Ken Boyer demonstrated his many leadership skills in 1964 when he helped St. Louis to its first World Series crown in 18 years. Boyer won MVP honors that season with a 24-homer, 119-RBI performance. In the Series, he delivered a momentum-turning grand slam in Game 4. A five-time Gold Glove winner who started four consecutive All-Star games (and played in 10), the highly professional Boyer had the respect not only of his teammates but of everyone in baseball. He batted higher than .300 five times, with his career-best mark of .329 coming in 1961. He ranks second to Stan Musial on the Cardinals' all-time home run list with 255.

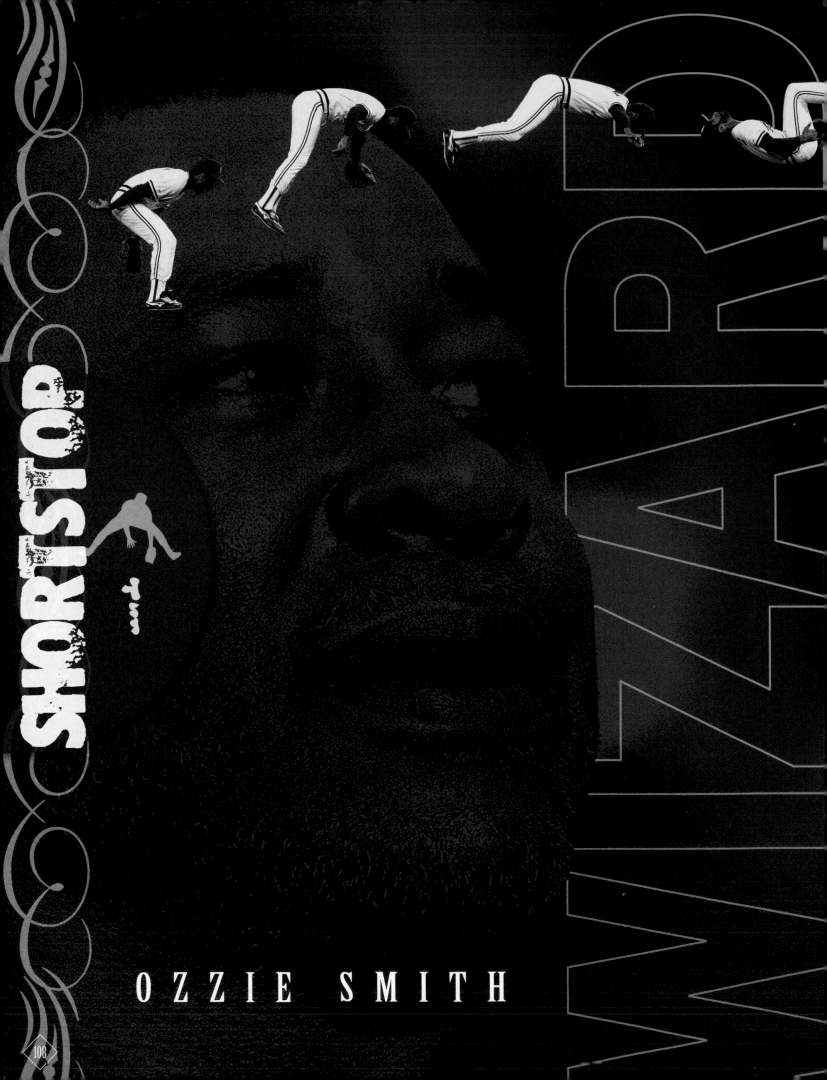

SHORTSTOP

WIZARD

OZZIE SMITH

hat Rogers Hornsby and Stan Musial were to offense, Ozzie Smith was to defense. As a Cardinal, Smith won 11 consecutive Gold Gloves beginning in 1982 and topped National League shortstops in fielding percentage seven times. Smith, who batted .211 for San Diego in 1979, made himself into a highly capable offensive player. In 1987, he helped the Cards to their third World Series appearance in six seasons with his airtight defense (only 10 errors) and solid offense (.303 average and 75 RBIs). Playing with a flair afield and exhibiting a keen insight into how all facets of the game should be played, Smith rates as one of the most popular players in Cardinals history. Besides his many fielding records, he is sixth on the franchise's all-time hits list and third among Cards basestealers.

LEFT FIELD
20

LOU
BROCK

ou Brock provided the spark at the top of the lineup that ignited the Cardinals to three pennants and two World Series titles in the 1960s. He led the National League in stolen bases eight times and established major league season and career steals records (both since broken). He is St. Louis' all-time steals leader and ranks No. 2 behind Stan Musial in six Cardinals career offensive categories—games played, runs, hits, total bases, at-bats and doubles. In 21 World Series games, he hit .391 and stole 14 bases.

Lou Brock

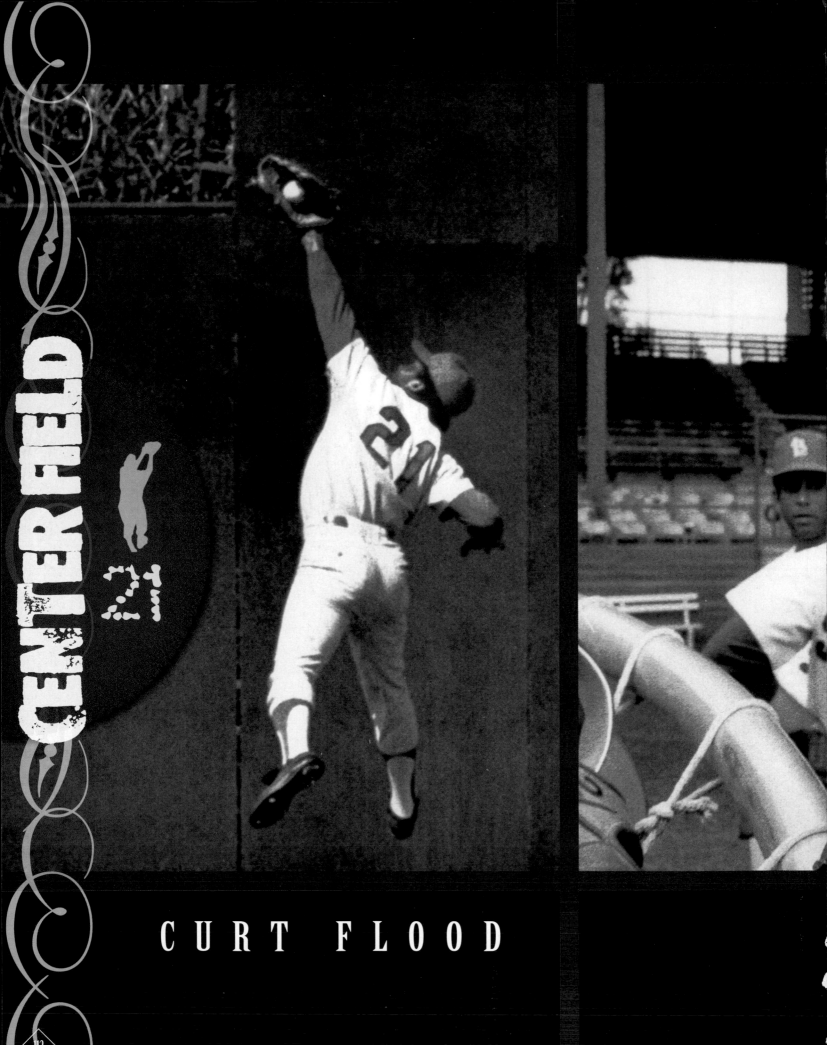

CENTER FIELD

21 *Two*

CURT FLOOD

urt Flood is perhaps best known for challenging baseball's reserve clause, but his accomplishments on the field were plenty. Flood won seven consecutive Gold Gloves, and in one stretch he played 226 games without an error. That flawless defensive streak included the entire 1966 season, during which he handled 396 chances without a miscue. Plus, Flood batted .300 or better six times, with highs of .335 in 1967 and .322 in 1961. A little man at 5-9 and 165 pounds, he reached double figures in home runs four times, had 70 or more RBIs three times and tied Pittsburgh's Roberto Clemente for the National League lead in hits with 211 in 1964.

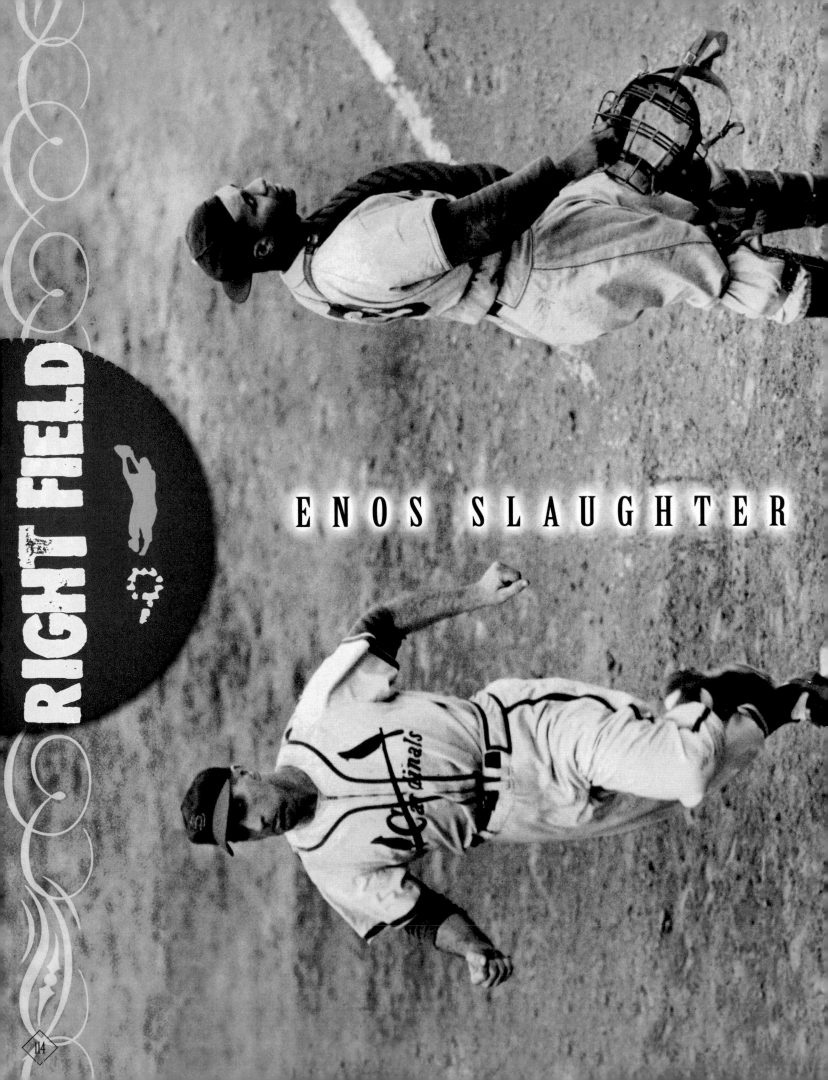

RIGHT FIELD

ENOS SLAUGHTER

Enos Slaughter played in 10 All-Star Games, and he batted .381 in the midsummer classic. "Country" hit .305 in his 13 seasons as a Cardinal, and he fashioned a .300 mark overall in 19 years as a major leaguer. Slaughter ranks in the top five in most offensive categories in Cardinals history. He is second only to Stan Musial in RBIs despite missing three prime years because of military service. And, of course, he will live forever in Cardinals lore because of his World Series-winning sprint around the bases in the 1946 World Series against the Boston Red Sox.

Ted Simmons' first full season as the Cardinals' No. 1 catcher was 1971, and his .304 average that season proved he could swing the bat. Simmons batted .300 or higher six times in 10 years of regular catching duty for St. Louis, a span in which he averaged 90 runs batted in and five times hit 20 or more home runs. He holds Cardinals records for most home runs and RBIs in a season by a catcher, hitting 26 homers in 1979 and driving in 96 runs in 1972. Simmons actually had two 100-RBI seasons for the Cards—1974 and 1975, years in which he also played at other positions. In '75, he finished second in the National League batting race with a career-high .332 mark. He appeared in three All-Star Games and was a member of the N.L. team six times overall.

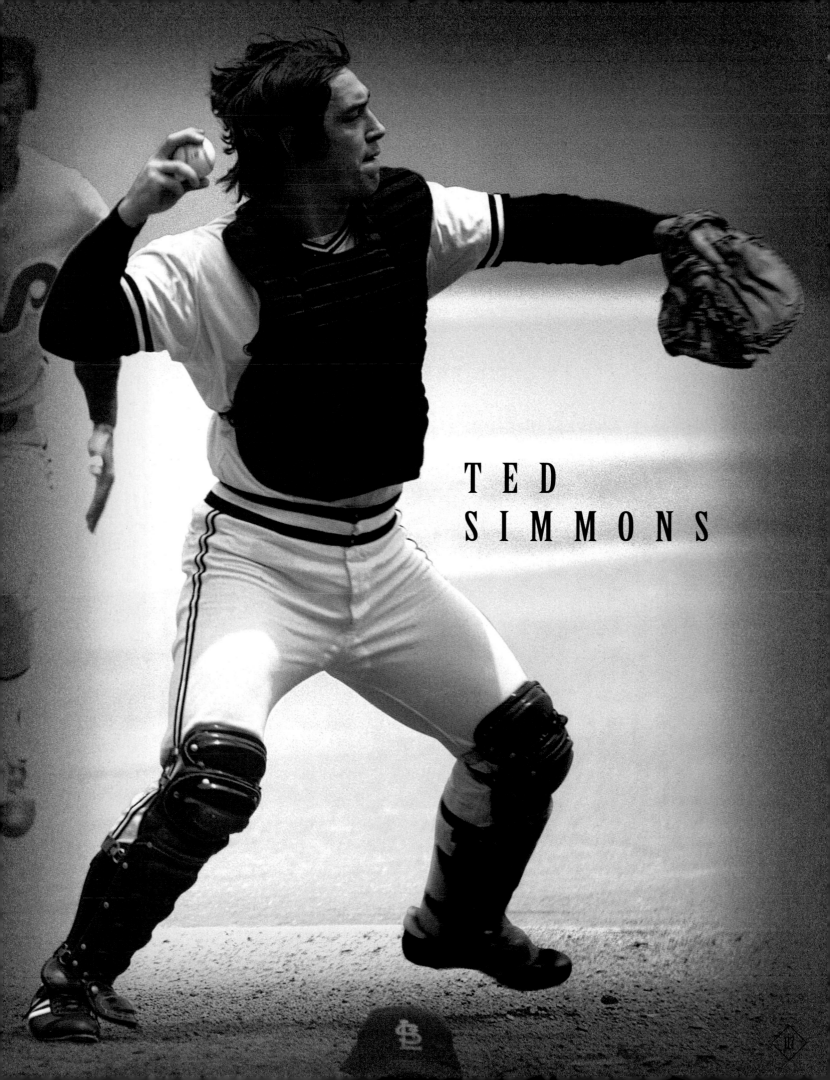

TED
SIMMONS

RH PITCHER
45

BOB GIBSON

There is little argument about Bob Gibson's ranking as the greatest Cardinals pitcher of all time. He won 251 games, put together five 20-victory seasons, captured two Cy Young Awards and one Most Valuable Player honor, pitched a no-hitter and recorded 3,117 strikeouts. In 1968, he set a major league record for lowest ERA, 300 or more innings pitched, finishing with a figure of 1.12. When games mattered the most, he came up big. Gibson compiled a 7-2 record in nine World Series starts and pitched eight complete games. His Series ERA was 1.89, and he struck out 92 batters in 81 innings. Seventeen of his strikeouts came in Game 1 of the 1968 Series. Gibson also won nine Gold Gloves.

LH PITCHER 31

HARRY BRECHEEN

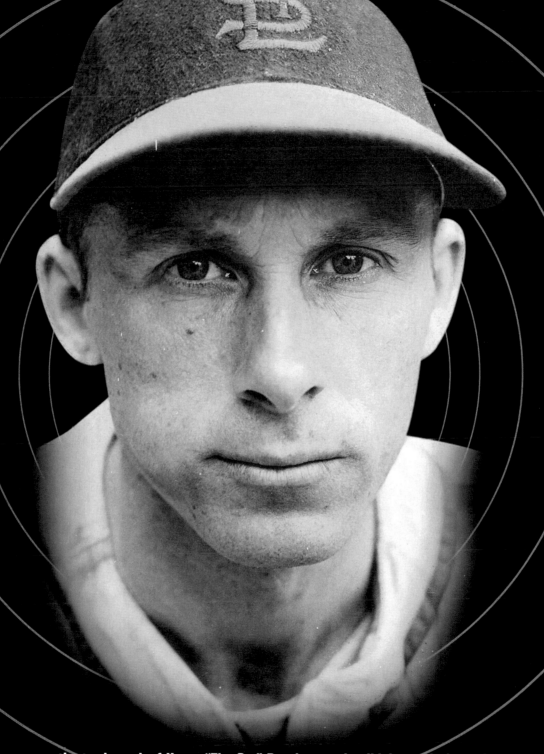

onsistency was the trademark of Harry "The Cat" Brecheen, who didn't reach the majors to stay until he was 28 years old but won 127 games in 10 full seasons with the Cardinals. From 1944 through 1949, Brecheen posted at least 14 victories each season. He was outstanding in 1948, winning 20 games and leading the National League in ERA (2.24), strikeouts (149) and shutouts (seven). His career winning percentage as a Cardinal was .617. He became the first lefthander to win three games in a World Series, accomplishing the feat in 1946 when he pitched two complete-game victories against the Red Sox and then won in relief in Game 7. His nickname derived from his cat-quick fielding skills.

CLOSER 42

fig.1 Split-finger Fastball

BRUCE SUTTER

There was no question about what was coming when relief pitcher extraordinaire Bruce Sutter was on the mound. The only uncertainty was whether the batter would be able to hit the pitch, a split-finger fastball. More often than not, Sutter came out the winner in the confrontation—and so did the Cardinals. In his four seasons with St. Louis, Sutter led the National League in saves three times (with a high of 45 in 1984). In the Cards' 1982 World Series championship season, he recorded 36 saves and got the final out in the Series by striking out Milwaukee's Gorman Thomas.

STEVE CARLTON

Cardinals pitching coach Howie Pollet thought so much of teenager Steve Carlton's potential in 1963 that he offered to pay Carlton's signing bonus out of his own pocket. That was just one indication that Carlton might be headed to stardom. Although most of his fame came after he left the Cardinals— the lefthander was traded to the Phillies in February 1972 after a contract dispute—he was a 20-game winner for the Cards in 1971 and notched 77 of his 329 career wins in a St. Louis uniform.

OTHER STARTERS

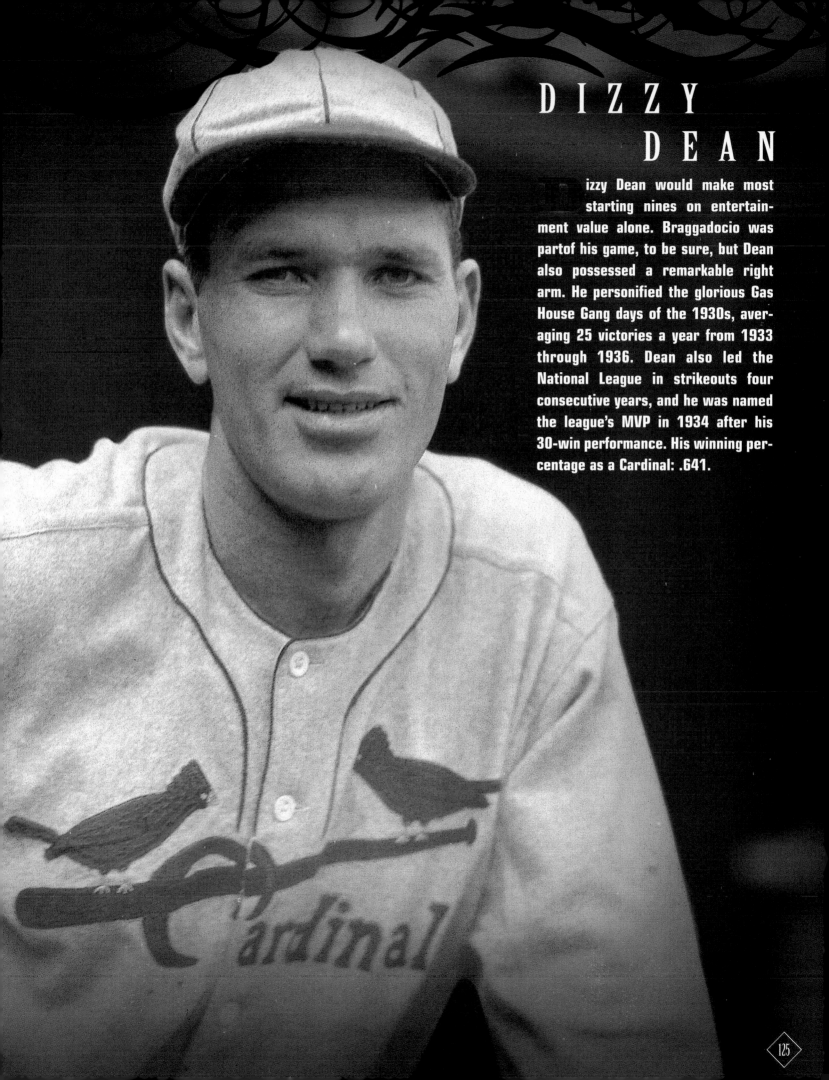

DIZZY DEAN

izzy Dean would make most starting nines on entertainment value alone. Braggadocio was part of his game, to be sure, but Dean also possessed a remarkable right arm. He personified the glorious Gas House Gang days of the 1930s, averaging 25 victories a year from 1933 through 1936. Dean also led the National League in strikeouts four consecutive years, and he was named the league's MVP in 1934 after his 30-win performance. His winning percentage as a Cardinal: .641.

The
Cardinals-Cubs
RIVALRY

Every winter, when the major league schedule is released for the upcoming season, certain games immediately draw attention.

For fans in St. Louis and Chicago, it's the no-holds-barred confrontations between the Cardinals and the Cubs.

Whether the scene is Busch Stadium or Wrigley Field, the rivalry is hot and heavy—not only between the teams, but their fans as well. And as soon as the schedule is made public, fans in each city gobble up tickets for Cardinals-Cubs games in their home parks—and for pilgrimages to the rival city. Thousands of fans make the trip up and down Interstate 55 for Cards-Cubs series each year—and some even pile into the car three times in the course of a season.

It is not unusual to see Wrigley Field bleacherites wearing T-shirts reading "I cheer for two teams, the Cubs and whoever is playing the Cardinals." At Busch Stadium, the message is reversed. There are almost as many fans decked out in blue as there are red in St. Louis, and the opposite is true in Chicago.

Fans from each town are well versed in the baseball lore of the other city, and they don't hesitate to point out the other team's shortcomings over and over again.

Cardinals fans know all about the exploits of Ernie Banks, Billy Williams, Ferguson Jenkins and Ryne Sandberg—and Hack Wilson, Stan Hack and Phil Cavarretta, for that matter. Cubs fans are all too familiar with Stan Musial, Bob Gibson, Ken Boyer and Ozzie Smith—and Dizzy Dean, Joe Medwick and Enos Slaughter, too.

St. Louis fans will tell you why they have a strong dislike for catcher Steve Swisher, even though he spent some time in a Cardinals uniform. Playing for

Longtime Cardinal Rogers Hornsby (top) didn't look quite right in a Cubs uniform. Outfielders Max Flack (immediate right) and Cliff Heathcote switched teams between games of a doubleheader.

the Cubs against the Pirates on the final day of the 1974 season, Swisher was charged with a ninth-inning passed ball that enabled Pittsburgh, trying to fight off the Cards for the East Division title, to tie the game. The Pirates then won in the 10th inning, clinching the division crown. A Pirates loss would have given the Cardinals a chance to force a tie for first place.

Cardinals fans still bemoan—and Cubs fans continue to cheer—that June day in 1984 when Sandberg hit two home runs off Bruce Sutter, one that tied the game in the ninth inning and another that deadlocked it in the 10th. Almost no one remembers that St. Louis' Willie McGee hit for the cycle in the same game, which the Cubs won in 11 innings.

No one on either side could tell you that the Cubs

Gas House Gang member Leo Durocher went on to manage the Cubs, a franchise that has never gotten over its 1964 trade of Lou Brock to the Cardinals.

were making a big mistake when they traded Lou Brock to the Cardinals in a six-player deal in 1964, with pitcher Ernie Broglio the principal player going to Chicago. Brock, of course, turned into a Hall of Famer and Broglio hurt his arm and won only seven games for the Cubs in three years. Fans of both teams reflect on the deal as fate—the kind that more often than not has favored the Cardinals.

Cubs-Cards games have been emotional—and historic. Musial collected his 3,000th career hit at Wrigley Field. Brock's 3,000th bounded off the hand of the Cubs' Dennis Lamp at Busch Stadium. Mark McGwire's record-breaking 62nd homer was against Chicago's Steve Trachsel at Busch.

There were epic pitching duels between Hall of Famers Gibson and Jenkins. Sutter and Lee Smith

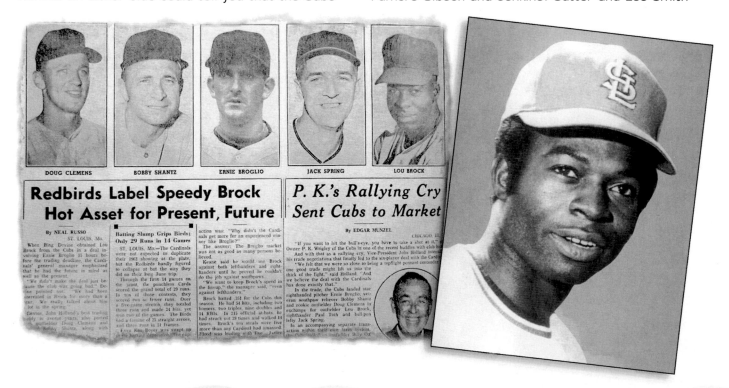

Bruce Sutter was congratulated countless times as the Cubs' closer—he won the N.L. Cy Young Award in 1979—and won high praise in the same role with St. Louis. He led the league in saves three times while pitching for the Cardinals.

Honored at Wrigley Field, Cardinals shortstop Ozzie Smith acknowledged the throng—which included pockets of red in the usually true-blue bleachers.

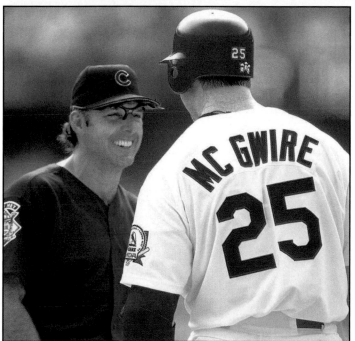

In the fierce battle of red vs. blue, friendships endure among the players—as St. Louis' Mark McGwire and Cardinal-turned-Cub Gary Gaetti proved.

saved games for both teams, and Rogers Hornsby showed his extraordinary batting prowess both as a Cardinal and a Cub. Harry Caray was a legend in both broadcasting booths.

Cubs-Cards meetings also have been fodder for trivia. Musial made his lone pitching appearance in the majors—he faced one batter—in a 1952 game against the Cubs. Between games of a 1922 Chicago-St. Louis doubleheader, the clubs swapped outfielders. Cliff Heathcote played for the Cardinals in the first game and was in the Cubs' lineup in the nightcap. Max Flack was a Cub in the opener, a Cardinal in the second game.

The St. Louis-Chicago rivalry really took root in the 1940s. People became more transient after World War II, and it was not uncommon to take trips from one city to the other. The ever-expanding radio broadcasts of both teams also increased the clubs' popularity—and in turn fueled the rivalry. Fans became more familiar with the personnel on the rival club.

The Cardinals' biggest rivals on the field during the

Whether it's Busch Stadium or Wrigley Field, diehard Cards and Cubs fans show their colors. Changing allegiances is unheard of—well, almost. Broadcaster Harry Caray (below) managed to make the switch in the course of calling Cardinals games for 25 years and Cubs games for 16 seasons.

The red-vs.-blue rivalry can get red-hot—as it did in a 1996 game at Busch Stadium when tempers flared after the Cardinals' Andy Benes hit the Cubs' Brian McRae with a pitch. Still, order was soon restored.

'40s were the Dodgers, because the two teams often battled for first place. But that rivalry never was as intense for the fans as the St. Louis-Chicago matchup.

The Cubs, who had won four pennants from 1929 through 1938, were evolving into lovable losers—big teddy bears that you could cuddle up with but seldom had to fear. They won the National League pennant in 1945, yes, but the franchise has had a mostly dismal history ever since. Cardinals fans poke fun at the Cubs' inability to reach the World Series—they haven't made it since '45—and take delight in noting the North Siders haven't won a Series since 1908.

Broadcaster Al Hrabosky, a former Cardinals pitcher, regularly points out that any team can have a bad century. Cubs fans can't counter with similar barbs.

The Cardinals have won four World Series and seven pennants since 1945.

One person who had to learn to root for the Cubs and not the Cardinals was Caray, the voice of the Cards for 25 seasons. Caray spent the last 16 years of his life cheering openly for the Cubs as their lead broadcaster. "Holy Cow!" was transformed into "Cubs win! Cubs win!"—but not often enough to please the Bleacher Bums.

Caray and the fans in Chicago and St. Louis haven't been the only ones affected by the fierce rivalry. Consider the households in central Illinois, many almost equidistant from Chicago and St. Louis. There, it is not unusual to find two people in a family cheering for the Cardinals and two pulling for the Cubs. In Champaign, Peoria, Decatur and other towns

across the state, wagers are won or lost and friend-ships made or broken because of the results of Cardinals-Cubs games.

Usually, there has been nothing more significant than pride riding on the outcome of a particular Cardinals-Cubs game or series. One notable exception was in 1935, when the Cubs and Cards battled for the National League pennant—and the Cubs clinched the flag with a victory in the first game of a doubleheader in St. Louis. The win was Chicago's 20th straight in the stretch run, a streak they extended to 21 in the nightcap.

Imagine, then, the intensity of the rivalry and the attendant media glare should the two Central Division franchises engage in another such heated fight for a championship. In view of the addition of the wild-card spot in the playoffs, it is even possible for the Cardinals and Cubs to be matched in the National League Championship Series—with a berth in the World Series on the line.

As Harry Caray would say, "Holy cow!"

The McGwire-Sammy Sosa homer race in '98 was a feel-good story for Cards and Cubs fans—and the nation.

The Unforgettables

Mark McGWIRE

Some trades in Cardinals history are easily forgotten. The deals didn't help the club to any sizable degree—or they benefited the other team. Many swaps have been of considerable significance; others are best relegated to the back pages of an encyclopedia. And, of course, there have been the blockbusters—the trades for Lou Brock and Ozzie Smith, among others.

One trade that will live forever in Cardinals lore occurred on July 31, 1997, when general manager Walt Jocketty swung a deal with the Oakland A's for first baseman Mark McGwire.

At the time of the trade, no one really knew quite what to make of it. The Cardinals had dispatched three promising pitchers—T.J. Mathews, Eric Ludwick and Blake Stein—to Oakland, but the Cards and their fans were certain of only one thing: McGwire would be in a Cardinals uniform for two months. Beyond that, it was anyone's guess.

McGwire was eligible to become a free agent after the 1997 season, and indications were strong that he wanted to be close to his Los Angeles-area home. Even though he had spent most of his major league career playing for Tony La Russa (named St. Louis manager in 1996), there was doubt that the strength of that relationship would be enough for Big Mac to make a long-term commitment to the Cardinals.

The CONTRACT

It took seven weeks for McGwire to decide against testing the free-agent market, and he signed a three-year contract with the Cardinals. At a news conference announcing the contract, McGwire became teary-eyed when he talked about one of the contract's provisions—a yearly $1 million donation to a foundation to help abused children.

That night, he went out and hit the longest home run in the 32-season history of Busch Stadium, a 517-foot shot.

The McGwire-St. Louis love affair had been consummated.

McGwire, who had hit 34 home runs in 105 games for the A's in '97, finished with 24 in 51 games with St. Louis. *Fifty-eight* home runs overall. Three shy of Roger Maris' single-season record.

No one really had any notion that the best was yet to come. But McGwire's two-month homer spree with the Cardinals had given fans plenty to talk about. They knew that if he stayed healthy, McGwire might pose a threat to Maris' mark in 1998.

The McGwire-St. Louis love affair had been consummated.

Chasing ROGER

McGwire tried to discourage such talk—with his words, not his bat. His opening-day salvo in '98 was a grand slam against the Dodgers, and he homered in his first four games of the season.

The McGwire moments then came at a furious clip. Fans collected memories—of a monstrous homer, or a long foul, or an upper-deck clout in batting practice. McGwire Mania forced people to stop and watch. Lines to the rest-rooms and concession stands vanished. The stadium grew quiet in anticipation. Flashbulbs popped. And when it was determined that McGwire likely had batted for the final time in a game, many people headed for the exits.

It would have been easy for the pressure to overwhelm McGwire, but he tried his best to ignore it. He said all the right things—about how his goal was to win as a team and that home runs were meaningful only if they contributed to a Cardinals victory.

His opening-day salvo in '98 was a grand slam against the Dodgers, and he homered in his first four games of the season.

61!

The home run total began to mount. McGwire twice hit three home runs in one game—in April and in May. He broke his own record for the longest homer at Busch Stadium, sending a rocket to dead center, an estimated 545 feet from home plate. He established a major league mark for most homers through May 31 (27) and through June 30 (37). At Bank One Ballpark in Phoenix, a radio station did live play-by-play while he took batting practice.

As the countdown to 61 picked up, McGwire grew a little testy, saying he felt like "a caged animal." Might the pressure be too great for him, after all?

Big Mac seemed to have some things working in his favor, though. The Cubs' Sammy Sosa had gone on a home run tear as well, and suddenly he was challenging McGwire for the league lead. McGwire relished the competition—it kept him focused and it also deflected some of the spotlight to Sosa. Also, McGwire appeared more relaxed after hitting home run No. 50 in New York on August 20. Reaching that plateau was a yearly goal, he acknowledged.

The home run assault remained steady, and after four homers in two games at Florida on September 1-2 lifted his season total to 59, McGwire hit No. 60 at Busch Stadium off the Reds' Dennys Reyes on September 5. He then smashed record-tying No. 61 at Busch against the Cubs' Mike Morgan on September 7.

He smashed record-tying No. 61 at Busch against the Cubs' Mike Morgan on September 7.

62!

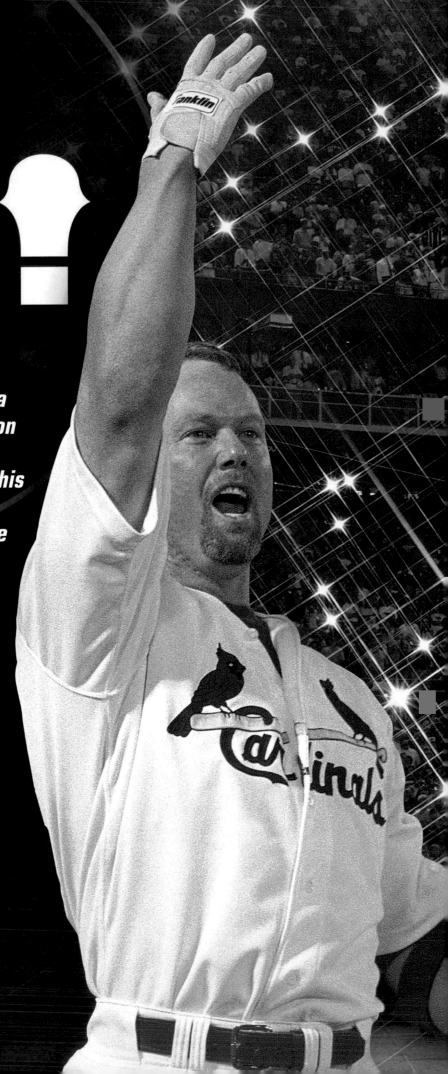

On September 8, 1998, with Sosa (58 homers and counting) looking on from right field, the record fell. McGwire's 62nd homer, ironically his shortest of the season at 341 feet, was a bullet down the left-field line off Steve Trachsel. It set off a frenzied celebration.

Most members of Maris' family were at the game, and McGwire went into the stands to give them a hug. His son Matt was there, and Matt joined his father in celebrating a moment that Cardinals fans thought belonged almost as much to them as to McGwire.

McGwire's embrace of Roger Maris' family tugged at the heartstrings.

70!

McGwire didn't stop there, of course. He went on to finish the season with 70 homers, the final two coming against Montreal on the last day of the season. As he exhaled after the season, McGwire admitted that he was in awe of himself.

Even though the record would fall three years later, to the Giants' Barry Bonds, nothing can take away from McGwire's accomplishments. He kept providing thrills, following with a 65-homer season in 1999, before injuries began to limit his effectiveness.

Farewell BIG MAC

When McGwire announced his retirement at the end of the 2001 season, the news was not unexpected. Although Big Mac left the game ranked No. 5 on the all-time list with 583 homers, many observers wondered what he could have done with good health on his side. Henry Aaron's record of 755, they said, might well have fallen.

One of those who preferred not to wonder—or look back—was McGwire himself. He didn't need the record to feel a great sense of satisfaction, to be happy with his accomplishments.

When Mark McGwire walked away from baseball, he was smiling.

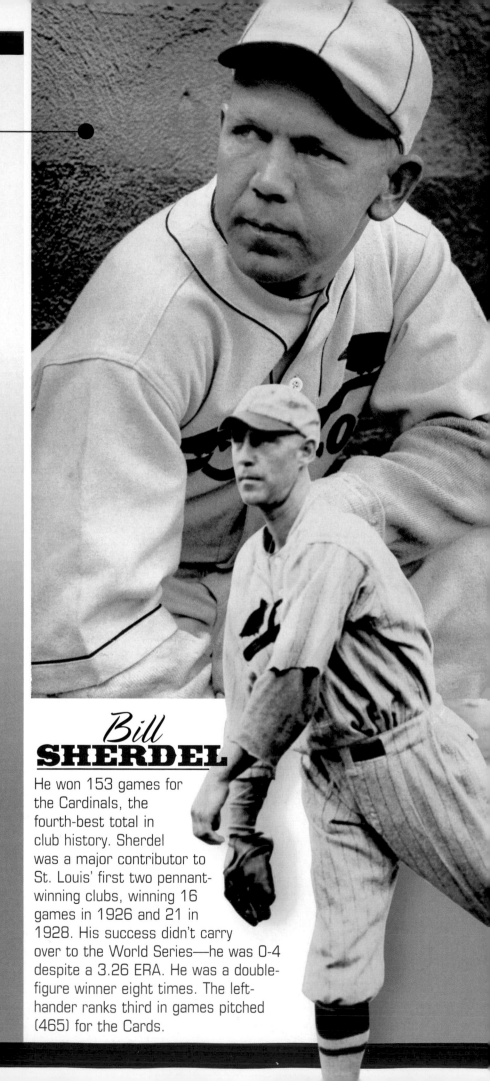

Bill
HALLAHAN

Nicknamed "Wild Bill," the lefthander led the league in walks three times— but also topped it in strikeouts twice. He was the N.L. starter and loser in the first All-Star Game (five walks in two-plus innings). He won 93 games in 10 seasons with the Cardinals, compiling 15-9 and 19-9 records in their pennant-winning seasons of 1930 and 1931. Hallahan pitched in seven games in four World Series, going 3-1 with a 1.36 ERA.

Bill
DOAK

He was known for throwing a spitball, but when he did it, the pitch was legal. Doak won 20 games in his first full year in the majors, 1914, and he compiled a National League-leading 1.72 ERA that season for the Cardinals. Seven years later, he again led the league in ERA. The righthander recorded 32 shutouts as a Cardinal, second on the all-time franchise list to Bob Gibson's 56.

Bill
SHERDEL

He won 153 games for the Cardinals, the fourth-best total in club history. Sherdel was a major contributor to St. Louis' first two pennant-winning clubs, winning 16 games in 1926 and 21 in 1928. His success didn't carry over to the World Series—he was 0-4 despite a 3.26 ERA. He was a double-figure winner eight times. The left-hander ranks third in games pitched (465) for the Cards.

Grover Cleveland
ALEXANDER

He spent only four of 20 major league seasons with the Cardinals but became a St. Louis legend because of his performance in the 1926 World Series (two victories and a dramatic relief outing in Game 7). Despite joining the Cards when he was 39 years old, Alexander went on to compile a 55-34 (.618) record for St. Louis and was a 21-game winner at age 40.

Bob
O'FARRELL

The catcher was named the National League's MVP in 1926, the Cardinals' first pennant-winning season. He ended the '26 World Series in stirring fashion, throwing out would-be basestealer Babe Ruth. His success and popularity helped earn O'Farrell the job as Cards player-manager the next season. St. Louis compiled a better record in 1927 under O'Farrell than in '26 under Rogers Hornsby, but the Cardinals lost out to the Pirates in a tight pennant race.

Branch
RICKEY

Although his playing and managerial records were not impressive, he became the architect of the Cardinals' winning ways. Rickey, who served the Cards in the front office from 1925 through 1942, was an astute judge of talent and a shrewd executive. Founder of the farm system, his skill in scouting and developing players was instrumental in the Cardinals' enormous success from 1926 through 1946, a period during which the Cards won nine pennants and six World Series.

Flint
RHEM

He was one of the Cardinals' more spirited players in late-1920s, showing a penchant for getting into off-field trouble and talking his way out of it. His best season was 1926, when he tied for the National League lead in victories with 20. He had three stints with the Cards, winning 81 games in his 10 seasons with the club. He was a member of St. Louis' pennant-winning teams of '26, 1928, 1930 and 1931. He also was briefly with the Cardinals' 1934 champions.

James "Rip"
COLLINS

He enjoyed his greatest season in 1934, helping the Gas House Gang to the World Series title. He tied for the league lead in homers that year with 35 and wound up second in RBIs with 128. He also had a robust .333 batting average. In the Series against the Tigers, Collins hit .367. In six seasons with the Cardinals, he batted .307 and drove in 516 runs. One of many outstanding first basemen in Cards history, he was sandwiched between Jim Bottomley and Johnny Mize in the lineage.

Terry MOORE

Called "Captain" by his teammates for his leadership on and off the field, Moore never received the acclaim he deserved outside his own clubhouse. The center fielder had no peers defensively, and he was a consistent offensive player—as his .280 batting average over 11 seasons attests. A four-time All-Star Game participant, he played between Stan Musial and Enos Slaughter in the 1940s in what some consider one of the greatest outfields of all time. He lost three years in his prime because of military service.

Paul DEAN

He is known more as Dizzy's brother than for his own accomplishments—which is a slight to his ability. He won 19 games in each of his first two seasons, 1934 and 1935, but at age 22 "Daffy" saw his promising career short-circuited because of an arm injury. He underwent surgery for torn cartilage and never regained the velocity on his fastball. Dean won only eight more games as a Cardinal.

Pepper MARTIN

One of the stars of the Gas House Gang because of his fiery play, Martin was always sliding, diving and hustling. As a rookie outfielder, he helped lead the Cardinals to the 1931 pennant, then was a sensation in the World Series. He also was a key performer on the 1934 World Series championship team, this time as the Cards' third baseman. Martin had a career .418 batting average in World Series play. He topped the National League in stolen bases three times in one four-year span.

Harry WALKER

Walker delivered the hit that sent Enos Slaughter tearing around the bases for the winning run in Game 7 of the 1946 World Series. He lost two seasons in his prime because of military duty and had a regular spot in a crowded Cardinals outfield for only two years. Traded to the Phillies early in the 1947 season, he won the National League batting title that year. He served as Cards manager for most of 1955.

Del RICE

He ranks second to Ted Simmons in games caught by a Cardinal. Only Rice and Simmons have logged more than 1,000 games behind the plate for the Cards. He spent 12 of his 17 big-league seasons with the Cardinals. Rice split time with Joe Garagiola early in his career, then settled in as a regular. Had 11 homers and 65 RBIs in 1952.

Joe GARAGIOLA

He gained fame as a broadcaster in part by poking fun at his playing ability. In fact, he was a decent player. As a 20-year-old Cards rookie, Garagiola batted .316 in the 1946 World Series and had four hits in Game 4. Except for a stint in the minors in 1948, he was a Cardinal until 1951, when he was traded to the Pirates in a seven-player deal. He also played for the Cubs and Giants. Was 28 when his playing career ended.

Billy SOUTHWORTH

As an outfielder, he helped the Cardinals to their first World Series title in 1926 after being acquired from the Giants.

As a manager, he directed the Cards to pennants in 1942, 1943 and 1944. He's the only two-time World Series winner ('42, '44) among Cardinals managers. In the five seasons from 1941 through 1945, Southworth's Cardinals won 508 games. He also was manager of the 1948 pennant-winning Boston Braves.

Whitey KUROWSKI

Kurowski overcame an arm injury to have a fine career. He was the regular third baseman on all four pennant-winning Cardinals teams of the 1940s. He hit a World Series-clinching home run in 1942, connecting for a two-run shot in the ninth inning of Game 5. Spent his entire nine-year major league career with the Cards. He batted .323 with 21 home runs and 102 RBIs in 1945. Hit 27 homers and drove in 104 runs in 1947. Kurowski played in three All-Star Games.

Marty MARION

He was named the National League's MVP in 1944 because of his superb play at shortstop and his leadership skills. Marion earned the nickname Mr. Shortstop because of his defensive skills. A seven-time All-Star, ranks second to Ozzie Smith for most games at shortstop in his Cardinals' career. Spent all 13 years as a player in St. Louis, 11 with Cardinals and two with Browns.

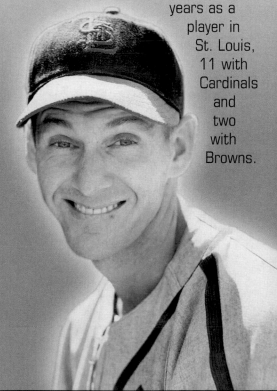

Ted WILKS

He had a sensational beginning to his Cardinals career, posting a 17-4 record as a starter/reliever in 1944 and then coming out of the bullpen in decisive Game 6 of the World Series to retire the Browns' final 11 batters. Wilks compiled a 12-0 mark over the 1946 and 1947 seasons, years in which he pitched almost exclusively in relief. He was 10-3 in '49. Wound up 51-20 as a Cardinal, 8-10 elsewhere.

Mort & Walker COOPER

Mort was the pitcher and Walker the catcher, and the Cooper brothers were a force for the Cards. Mort was the N.L. MVP in 1942, going 22-7 with a league-low 1.78 ERA. Walker hit .281 that year. From '42 through '44, Mort was 65-22. Walker hit .318 in 1943 and .317 in 1944. Playing despite the death of their father earlier in the day, the Coopers formed the Cards' battery in Game 2 of the 1943 World Series. Mort won, 4-3.

George KISSELL

The former minor league infielder never played in the majors, but he has been crucial in the development of Cardinals players since the 1940s. Most of his time has been spent as a manager or special instructor in the Cards' farm system. It was low-profile work but helped produce quality players at the big-league level. He also has been a Cardinals coach and a player-development coordinator.

Tom ALSTON

Alston was the first black player to see action for the Cardinals, breaking into the big leagues with St. Louis on April 13, 1954—seven years after modern major league baseball had been integrated. The lanky first baseman, coming off a strong season in the Pacific Coast League, appeared in 66 games in '54, batting .246 with four homers. He saw brief duty with the Cardinals in each of the next three seasons.

Howie POLLET

The lefthander won 21 games for St. Louis in 1946 and 20 in 1949. His final victory in '46 was an important one—it came in the opening game of a best-of-three pennant playoff with Brooklyn. He led the N.L. in earned-run average in 1943, went away to military duty the next two seasons and then won another ERA crown in his first season back. Pollet was 97-65 in nine seasons with the Cardinals. He later served as pitching coach for the Cards.

Hemus succeeded Marty Marion as the Cards' No. 1 short-stop in 1951. Played a key role in the team's greatest comeback—from an 11-0 deficit against the Giants in 1952. Hemus' eighth-inning homer tied the score and his two-run shot in the ninth provid-ed the ultimate margin of vic-tory in a 14-12 win. He man-aged the team for 2½ sea-sons, beginning in 1959.

Lindy
McDANIEL

The Cardinals' first star closer. He made 55 or more relief appearances for St. Louis from 1959 through 1962. In 1960, he compiled a 12-4 record, 2.09 ERA and 26 saves (not yet an official statistic). McDaniel spent 21 seasons in the majors; was 66-54 in his eight years with the Cards. He was the older brother of Von McDaniel, one of team's greatest pitching prospects. Von's career ended abruptly because of an arm injury.

Julian
JAVIER

Slick-fielding second baseman was a key player on the Cardinals' three pennant-winning teams in the 1960s. Javier was strong offensively in the Cards' championship season of 1967, hit-ting .281 with 14 homers and 64 runs batted in. He hit .346 for St. Louis in 15 World Series games. Stole 26 bases in 1962. Holds Cardinals career record for most games played at second base, outdistancing even Red Schoendienst. Ended his career with the Reds after 12 seasons as a Cardinal.

Orlando *CEPEDA*

Cepeda was a Cardinal for only two full seasons, but they were magical years. Obtained from the Giants in May 1966, "Cha-Cha" was named N.L. MVP award in 1967 after leading "El Birdos" to the pennant. He hit .325 with 25 homers and a league-high 111 RBIs for St. Louis, which went on to defeat Boston in the World Series. Cepeda fell off in '68 but still helped the Cards win back-to-back pennants for the first time since '43 and '44.

Curt *SIMMONS*

Signed in May 1960 after being released by the Phillies, he helped solidify the Cardinals' rotation. He was at his best in 1963 and 1964. In '63, he fashioned a 15-9 record and a 2.48 ERA. At age 35, he won 18 games for the '64 Cards, who went on to capture St. Louis' first World Series title in 18 years. Although best known because of his success with Philadelphia, Simmons was 69-58 for the Cards with a 3.25 ERA.

Larry *JACKSON*

Was a consistent, gritty pitcher for the Cardinals, posting victory totals of 15, 13, 14, 18, 14 and 16 from 1957 through 1962. He worked a National League-leading 282 innings in 1960, a year in which he made a league-high 38 starts. Traded to the Cubs after the '62 season, he won 24 games for Chicago in 1964—and lost 21 in 1965. He was a double-figure winner and loser in each of his final 11 major league seasons.

Roger MARIS

Playing for the Yankees, he achieved what once seemed impossible—he broke Babe Ruth's single-season home run record. Yet Maris often said his most enjoyable years were spent with the Cardinals. Maris was a Cardinal in 1967 and 1968, years in which the outfielder was an integral part of pennant-winning teams. In St. Louis' seven-game victory over Boston in the '67 World Series, he hit .385 and drove in seven runs.

Mike SHANNON

The St. Louis native was a Cardinal for nine seasons. He broke into the starting lineup in the Cards' championship season of 1964. St. Louis' No. 1 right fielder through 1966, he moved to third base when the Cardinals traded for Roger Maris. In the Cards' pennant-winning seasons of 1967 and 1968, he had RBI totals of 77 and 79. A kidney ailment forced his retirement. A crowd favorite as a player, he is highly popular as a Cards broadcaster.

Bill WHITE

White hit 20 or more homers for St. Louis from 1961 through 1965 and topped the 100-RBI mark three straight seasons. In '61, he tied Ty Cobb's big-league record of 14 hits in two consecutive doubleheaders. Also excelled afield—he won six Gold Gloves in a row as the Cards' first baseman. Played in six All-Star Games as a member of the Cardinals. Traded to the Phillies after the 1965 season, he returned to the Cards briefly in 1969. Served as National League president from 1989 to 1994.

Tim
McCARVER

He was a rarity—a four-decade major leaguer. McCarver made his debut at age 17, getting into eight games with the 1959 Cardinals, and he bowed out with the Phillies in 1980. Played 12 of his 21 seasons for the Cardinals. Reliable and durable, he was a heady catcher and a tough hitter on St. Louis' standout 1964, 1967 and 1968 teams. He batted .478 in the '64 World Series and .333 in the '68 Series.

Ernie
BROGLIO

Broglio will live forever in Cardinals lore as the key man who went to the Cubs in the six-player 1964 trade that brought Lou Brock to St. Louis. The righthanded pitcher, soon beset by arm problems, proved a bust in Chicago and Brock evolved into a Hall of Famer for the Cards, but most people forget how good Broglio was as a Cardinal. In 1960, he won 21 games and had a 2.74 ERA; in 1963, he was 18-8.

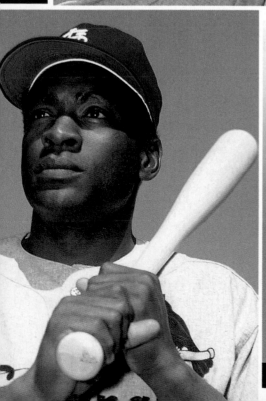

Dal
MAXVILL

Never an offensive threat, Maxvill nevertheless was a good fit on successful Cardinals teams of his era. The shortstop was a Gold Glove winner in 1968 and made only 13 errors in both 1970 and 1971. He started all 21 games of the 1964, 1967 and 1968 World Series—in the '64 Series against the Yankees, Maxvill replaced the injured Julian Javier at second base. He served as general manager of the Cardinals from 1985 to 1994.

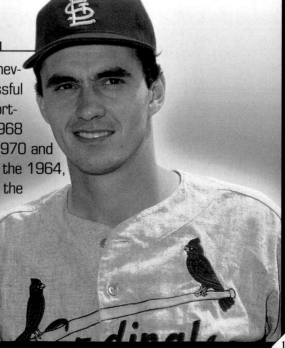

Dick ALLEN

He spent only one season in St. Louis, 1970, but it was a memorable year. Obtained in the deal that sent Curt Flood and Tim McCarver to the Phillies, Allen hit 34 home runs, drove in 101 runs and started at first base for the National League in the All-Star Game. His home run total was the highest by a Cardinals player since Stan Musial hit 35 in 1954, and no Cardinal would hit more until Jack Clark connected for 35 in 1987.

John DENNY

He won his greatest fame after leaving the Cardinals, capturing the National League's Cy Young Award in 1983 while pitching for the Phillies. Still, Denny topped the N.L. in earned-run average while pitching for the Cards—he led with a figure of 2.52 in 1976—and was a double-figure winner three times for St. Louis. In 1978, he won a team-high 14 games and had a 2.96 ERA. Spent six seasons with the Cardinals and went 51-46.

Bake McBRIDE

Was the N.L. Rookie of the Year in 1974 after hitting .309 with 30 stolen bases. His steals total almost went unnoticed—Lou Brock had 118. The fleet McBride scored the winning run in the longest game in Cardinals history—a 25-inning marathon against the Mets in 1974. He led off the 25th with an infield single, raced to third on a botched pickoff attempt and scored when a throw to the plate was dropped. Hit .307 for the Cards over five seasons.

Joe TORRE

Enjoyed one of the finest seasons in Cardinals history in 1971, winning the National League batting title with a .363 average and leading the league with 137 RBIs. It was an N.L. MVP season for Torre, who had 24 homers and a league-best 230 hits. Played third base in '71 but also was a first baseman and catcher as a Cardinal. He hit .308 for St. Louis over six seasons. Managed the club from 1990 to 1995.

Bob FORSCH

Earned his spot in club history by becoming the only Cardinals pitcher to throw two no-hitters (vs. the Phillies in 1978, the Expos in 1983). He accomplished a lot more, though—he was a double-figure winner 10 times for the Cards and ranks third in franchise wins with 163. Was a 20-game winner in 1977. Forsch is third on the Cards' all-time strikeout list and fourth in games pitched.

Al HRABOSKY

The "Mad Hungarian" was entertaining even before throwing a pitch, psyching himself up near the mound and then storming to the rubber to face a hitter. Was at his dramatic best in a national-TV game on the night of May 9, 1977, when he struck out the Reds' George Foster, Johnny Bench and Bob Bailey with the bases full in the ninth inning of a tie game. Cards won in the 10th. Led the team in saves four straight years. In '75, he was 13-3 with a 1.67 ERA and shared the N.L. lead with 22 saves.

Keith
HERNANDEZ

One of the best defensive first basemen in the game's history, he won five
consecutive Gold Gloves as a Cardinal
and 11 in a row overall. Hernandez
shared the 1979 MVP award with
Pittsburgh's Willie Stargell after leading the league with a .344 average.
That marked the first of three straight
.300-plus years. He came up big in the
'82 World Series win over Milwaukee,
delivering a game-tying single in Game
7 and driving in eight runs overall.

Willie
McGEE

A virtual unknown when acquired
from the Yankees' organization in October 1981,
he became one of
the most beloved
players in fran-
chise history.
Called up
from the
minors in
1982,
McGee
helped the
Cardinals to
the pennant and
had a sterling
World Series that
included a two-
homer game and
great defensive play.
Was the league MVP
in 1985; won N.L.
batting title in '85
and 1990. Had
two stints with
the Cardinals
totaling 13
seasons.

Garry
TEMPLETON

When shortstop Templeton was traded to
San Diego for Ozzie Smith before the
1982 season, some thought the Padres
wound up with the better all-around player.
Templeton did possess great ability—he
had two 200-hit years with the Cardinals,
was the first switch hitter in the majors to
get 100 hits from each side of the plate in
one season and led the N.L. in triples
three consecutive years. Whitey Herzog
always raved about his sheer talent.

Todd
WORRELL

He ranks second on the Cardinals' all-time saves list with 129, having recorded 101 saves over a three-year span (1986 through 1988). He was selected the National League's Rookie of the Year in '86 when he had a league-leading 36 saves and a 2.08 ERA. Had two saves in the 1987 World Series. Encountered major physical problems beginning in the late-1980s, but he rebounded with strong seasons (1995, 1996) with the Dodgers near the end of his career.

George
HENDRICK

He was called "Silent George" because he wouldn't talk with the media. But he wasn't silent with his bat. Hendrick led the Cards in home runs four seasons in a row and in runs batted in five straight years (twice topping the 100-RBI mark). Got what proved to be the game winning hit in Game 7 of the 1982 World Series. Helped the Cardinals even as he left—he was traded to Pittsburgh in the deal that brought John Tudor to St. Louis.

Vince
COLEMAN

Was a key player on Cardinals teams of the mid-to-late 1980s. Stole 110 bases in 1985, a major league record for a rookie, en route to N.L. Rookie of the Year honors. Topped the 100-steal mark again in the next two years and led the N.L. six straight seasons. Was the victim of a freak accident before Game 4 of the 1985 NLCS, injuring his leg when run over by an automatic tarpaulin. Missed the rest of the '85 postseason.

Tommy HERR

The second baseman proved you don't have to be a power hitter to drive in runs—he had a 110-RBI season in 1985 despite hitting only eight home runs. Was a standout run-producer again in 1987, knocking in 83 runs during a season in which he had only two homers and 31 extra-base hits. Signed as an undrafted free agent, he made his Cardinals debut in 1979—on the night Lou Brock got his 3,000th hit. Had only 54 errors from 1981 through 1987. Was dealt to the Twins in 1988.

John TUDOR

Holds Cardinals records for best career winning percentage (.705) and ERA (2.52). After a 1-7 start in 1985, Tudor won 20 of last 21 decisions. Led the league with 10 shutouts in '85 and finished with a 1.93 ERA. Never a hard thrower, he relied on location and an excellent changeup. Dealt to the Dodgers in 1988, he returned to the Cards in 1990 and went 12-4.

Joaquin ANDUJAR

Andujar won 20 games in 1984 and 21 in 1985, becoming the first Cardinal to win 20 in consecutive seasons since Bob Gibson (1969, 1970). He was outstanding in 1982, too—as a 2.47 ERA attests. He often said that baseball was so unpredictable that it could be described in one word—"youneverknow." Won two games in the '82 World Series, including the clincher. He was ejected in Game 7 of the 1985 Series in Kansas City and traded to the Oakland A's six weeks later.

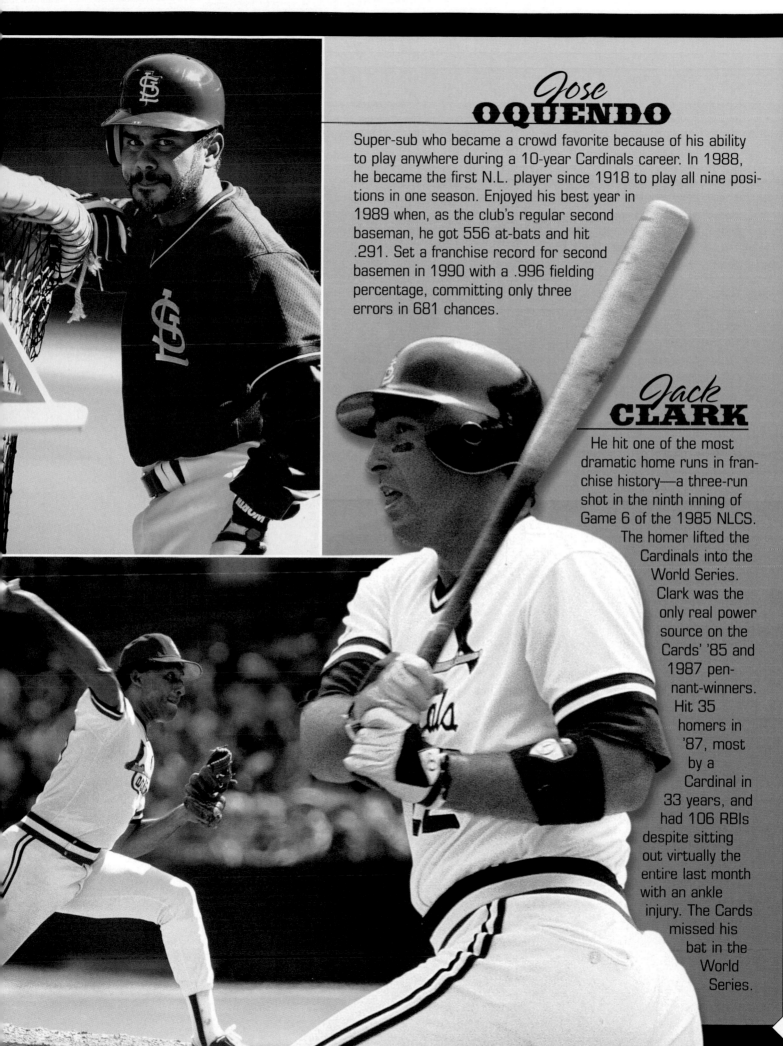

Jose OQUENDO

Super-sub who became a crowd favorite because of his ability to play anywhere during a 10-year Cardinals career. In 1988, he became the first N.L. player since 1918 to play all nine positions in one season. Enjoyed his best year in 1989 when, as the club's regular second baseman, he got 556 at-bats and hit .291. Set a franchise record for second basemen in 1990 with a .996 fielding percentage, committing only three errors in 681 chances.

Jack CLARK

He hit one of the most dramatic home runs in franchise history—a three-run shot in the ninth inning of Game 6 of the 1985 NLCS. The homer lifted the Cardinals into the World Series. Clark was the only real power source on the Cards' '85 and 1987 pennant-winners. Hit 35 homers in '87, most by a Cardinal in 33 years, and had 106 RBIs despite sitting out virtually the entire last month with an ankle injury. The Cards missed his bat in the World Series.

Darrell PORTER

He had been Whitey Herzog's catcher in Kansas City, and Herzog and the Cardinals lured the free agent to St. Louis in December 1980. Replacing the popular Ted Simmons, who had been traded, Porter did little to win over fans in 1981—but 1982 was a different story. He won MVP honors in both the '82 NLCS (.556 batting average) and the World Series (.286, five RBIs). Was a Cardinal for five seasons.

Terry PENDLETON

He drove in 96 runs in 1987, helping the Cardinals win the pennant. In the heat of the race, he hit a tying two-run, two-out homer in the ninth inning of a key September game at Shea Stadium. The Cards beat the Mets in the 10th. Won two Gold Gloves as a Cardinal. Seven-year stint with St. Louis got off to a fast start when he hit .324 in 67 games in 1984.

Ray LANKFORD

He had 20 or more home runs six times for the Cardinals. Was an offensive force in 1997 and 1998, hitting 31 homers each season and driving in a total of 203 runs. He became the first Cardinal to hit 30 homers in consecutive years since Stan Musial (1954, 1955). Lankford is third on the Cardinals' all-time home run list with 222 and No. 1 in career homers at Busch Stadium with 120.

Albert **PUJOLS**

Was a unanimous pick for 2001 Rookie of the Year in the National League after turning in one of the best seasons by any player in Cardinals history. His 130 RBIs established an N.L. rookie record. Pujols hit 37 home runs, shattering the Cards' rookie mark, and he finished sixth in the league batting race with a .329 average. At age 21, he played his way onto the roster in spring training and proved versatile. Played the outfield, third base and first base.

Rick **ANKIEL**

Ankiel showed outstanding promise in the 2000 regular season by winning 11 games for the Cardinals as a 21-year-old rookie. He finished second in the Rookie of the Year balloting. Established a Cardinals rookie record with 194 strikeouts, breaking the mark of 191 set by Dizzy Dean in 1932. A wild streak in the 2000 postseason posed a setback for the lefthander, and his inability to find the plate carried over to the 2001 season. He reached the majors in August 1999. A good hitter.

The BALLPARKS

Where Mike Shannon's 1964 World Series homer bounced off scoreboard

Where one-armed outfielder Pete Gray made big-league debut for Browns, April 17, 1945

Basepaths where Enos Slaughter made his Mad Dash to win seventh game of 1946 World Series

Landing point for final-day, ninth-inning grand slam by Hank Greenberg that gave Tigers 6-3 win over Browns and 1945 A.L. pennant

Cardinals brought 10 pennants, seven championships to Sportsman's Park

MVP Ken Boyer led Cardinals to 1964 pennant; Bob Gibson secured World Series championship with Game 7 win over Yankees

Where Browns' Bob Cain outdueled Indians star Bob Feller 1-0 in double one-hitter, April 23, 1952

STAN THE MAN MUSIAL: Cardinals' three-time MVP, seven-time batting champ collected 3,630 career hits, fourth all-time

Musial goes crazy: five home runs, nine RBIs in doubleheader vs. Giants, May 2, 1954

Browns' Bobo Holloman fires no-hitter in first major league start, May 6, 1953

Sportsman's
PARK
1892-1966

Point where Max West's All-Star Game-deciding home run landed in 1940

Point where one of Babe Ruth's three Game 4 home runs cleared bleachers in 1926 World Series, breaking auto dealer's window across Grand Avenue

A screen ran from the top of the fence to the roof of the right field pavilion

Great defensive shortstop Marty Marion wins 1944 MVP, Cardinals defeat Browns in World Series— the only all-St. Louis fall classic

Chet Laabs homers twice, Browns beat Yankees 5-2 and win only A.L. pennant, Oct. 1, 1944

A long line of great Cardinals second basemen: Rogers Hornsby, Frank Frisch, Red Schoendienst, Julian Javier

Browns first baseman George Sisler (right) batted .420 and compiled 41-game hitting streak in 1922; six-time Cardinals batting champ Rogers Hornsby hit .424 in 1924

Dean brothers, Dizzy and Paul, combined for 49 wins in 1934

DIZZY DEAN: Cardinals clinched pennant on final day of 1934 season—Dean won No. 30 that afternoon, beating Reds, 9-0

Ty Cobb, Tigers' 38-year-old player-manager, hits 3 homers, double, 2 singles and drives in 5 runs in 14-8 win over Browns, May 5, 1925

Batter's box where Eddie Gaedel, Bill Veeck's midget, drew walk in surprise appearance vs. Tigers, Aug. 19, 1951

Fans manage Browns in another Veeck promotional stunt, Aug. 24, 1951

St. Louis had a National League team in 1876, the league's first season, and again in 1877. After dropping out of the N.L., the city resurfaced as a league member in 1885 and 1886, only to see its team disband once more.

It was in 1892 that the Cardinals lineage began. That year, four teams from the American Association (a major league from 1882 through 1891) joined the National League. One of those franchises was owner Chris Von der Ahe's St. Louis Browns, who eventually were renamed the Perfectos and then the Cardinals.

That 1892 team played its first season at Grand Avenue and Dodier Street, where numerous struc-

tures called Sportsman's Park, with different configurations, would exist over the years. From 1893 through June 1920, the club played at Robison Field (Natural Bridge and Vandeventer avenues).

With the American League's St. Louis Browns owning Sportsman's Park until 1953—they first played at Grand and Dodier in 1902—and the Cardinals serving as tenants beginning in July 1920, Sportsman's played host to major league baseball through May 8, 1966. In early 1953, when Anheuser-Busch Inc. purchased the Cardinals and the ballpark, the facility was renamed Busch Stadium. (After the '53 season, the Browns moved to Baltimore.)

When the Cardinals moved into new Busch Memorial Stadium in 1966, August A. Busch Jr. donated the Sportsman's site to the Herbert Hoover Boys and Girls Club. The old park's stands and infrastructure are gone, but part of what was the field area remains.

First game at Grand and Dodier site: April 12, 1892. The Cardinals (Browns at the time) lost to Chicago, 14-10.

Final game: May 8, 1966. The Cardinals lost to the Giants, 10-5.

Site of 10 World Series (1926, '28, '30, '31, '34, '42, '43, '44, '46, and '64).

Site of 3 All-Star Games (1940, '48 and '57).

N.L. prevails 2-1 on 105-degree afternoon in hotly contested All-Star Game, July 12, 1966

Landing areas for Mark McGwire homers Nos. 62 and 70 during historic 1998 season

SOUTHWEST AIRLINES

KEITH HERNANDEZ: 1979 co-MVP and big gun in 1982 World Series championship

Where Curt Flood misjudged Jim Northrup's fly ball, opening gates to seventh-game Tigers win in 1968 World Series

Mark McGwire hits career homer No. 500 (Aug. 5, 1999), follows up record-breaking 1998 season with 65

Tom Lawless' second homer as a major leaguer, a three-run shot, helps Cardinals beat Twins and Frank Viola in Game 4 of 1987 World Series

OZZIE SMITH: The Wizard of Oz performed magic on left side of Cardinals' infield from 1982-96

Where Al Hrabosky, the "Mad Hungarian," meditated before striking out another batter

Steve Carlton strikes out 19 Mets but loses game 4-3, Sept. 15, 1969

Busch
STADIUM
1966-present

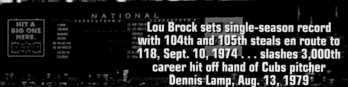

Lou Brock sets single-season record with 104th and 105th steals en route to 118, Sept. 10, 1974 . . . slashes 3,000th career hit off hand of Cubs pitcher Dennis Lamp, Aug. 13, 1979

Ozzie Smith's first lefthanded homer as a major leaguer shocks Dodgers in Game 5 of 1985 NLCS

BOB GIBSON: Five-time 20-game winner, two Cy Youngs, 1.12 ERA in 1968

Where Mark McGwire's 545-foot blast off Marlins' Livan Hernandez dented sign, May 16, 1998

Site of Gibson's overpowering 17-strikeout performance in Game 1 of 1968 World Series vs. Tigers

Roosting place of "Cha Cha" Cepeda, MVP cheerleader for 1967 El Birdos

Where Larry Jaster shut out Dodgers for fifth straight time in remarkable 1966 performance, Sept. 28

Where Vince Coleman, the Cardinals' 110-steal rookie, was gobbled up by automatic tarp before Game 4 of NLCS, Oct. 13, 1985

Line drive by Pirates slugger Roberto Clemente breaks Gibson's leg, July 15, 1967

The stadium was named for August A. Busch Jr., longtime chairman of Anheuser-Busch Inc., which owned the Cardinals from 1953 to 1995. First known as Busch Memorial Stadium, this is actually the second *Busch Stadium*. Sportsman's Park, the Cards' home field from mid-1920 to May 1966, was renamed Busch Stadium in '53 after the brewery purchased both the Cardinals franchise and the ballpark. Previously, the Cards had been Sportsman's Park tenants of the American League's St. Louis Browns.

Known as a turf stadium, the new Busch had natural grass as its first surface when it opened in 1966. The grass was in place through 1969, then replaced with artificial turf for the 1970 season.

The synthetic surface remained through 1995 before the return of natural grass in 1996.

The stadium's most popular feature isn't within its confines. Outside the northeast section stands a tall bronze statue of Stan Musial. "Stan" has become the meeting place for countless fans. In recent years, other Cardinals greats have been honored with statues in the Plaza of Champions.

■ **First game:** May 12, 1966, a 4-3 Cardinals win over Atlanta in 12 innings. The Braves' Felipe Alou hit the first home run in the ballpark—in fact, he hit two that night.

■ Site of five World Series (1967, '68, '82, '85 and '87).

■ Site of one All-Star Game (1966).

Scene of 1982 World Series victory.

The
GREATEST
MOMENTS

62

Roger Maris' major league record of 61 home runs in one season had stood for 37 years, and it really had not been threatened during that span. In the summer of 1998, however, Mark McGwire and the Cubs' Sammy Sosa came charging after Maris' mark, and when McGwire reached 62 on September 8 with a two-out, bases-empty homer in the fourth inning off the Cubs' Steve Trachsel at Busch Stadium, the baseball world erupted in celebration. Ironically, the home run—it was measured at 341 feet—was McGwire's shortest of the season.

1
McGwire Breaks Single-Season Home Run Record

— September 8, 1998 —

2

Enos Slaughter's Mad Dash

— October 15, 1946 —

The Cardinals and Red Sox were tied, 3-3, in Game 7 of the 1946 World Series when Enos Slaughter led off the bottom of the eighth inning with a single. He was still at first base two outs later when Harry Walker went to the plate for St. Louis. Walker hit a shot over shortstop Johnny Pesky's head into left-center. Slaughter took off, rounding second and heading for third. Center fielder Leon Culberson fielded the smash and threw to Pesky, who hesitated in making his relay to the plate—a throw that drew Red Sox catcher Roy Partee up the third-base line. Slaughter was home free. The Cards won, 4-3—Walker's hit was ruled a double—and were Series champions for the third time in five seasons.

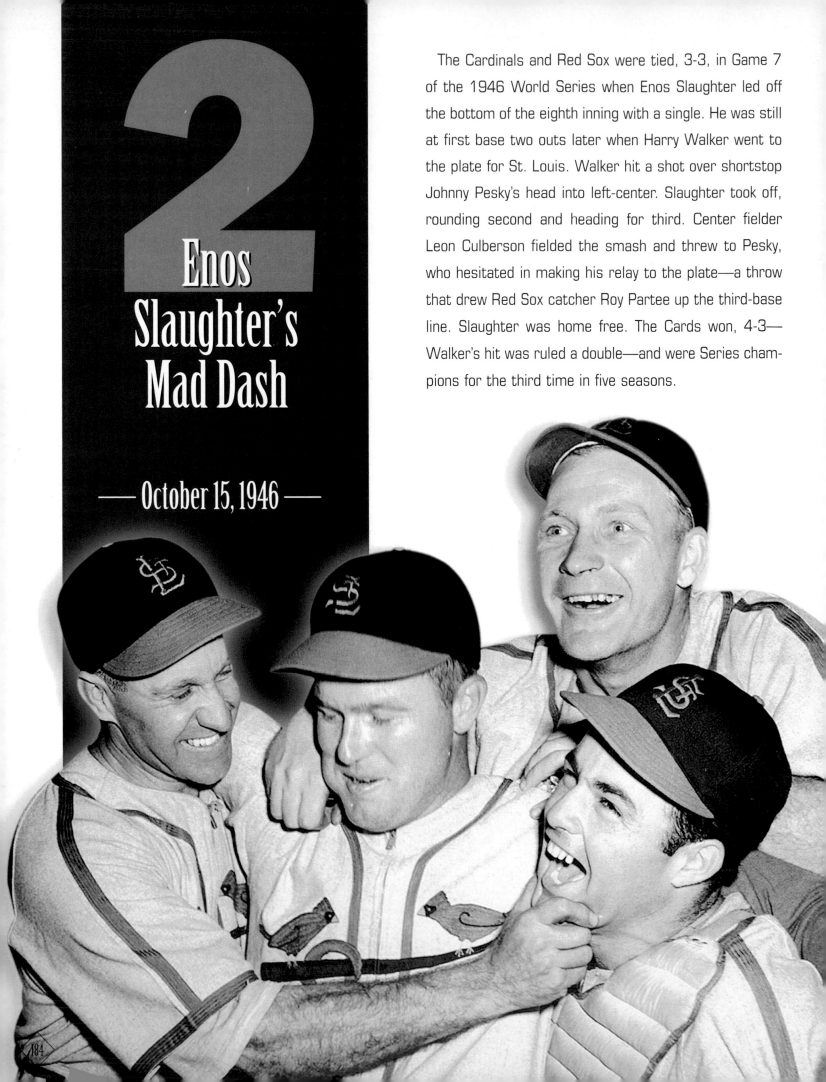

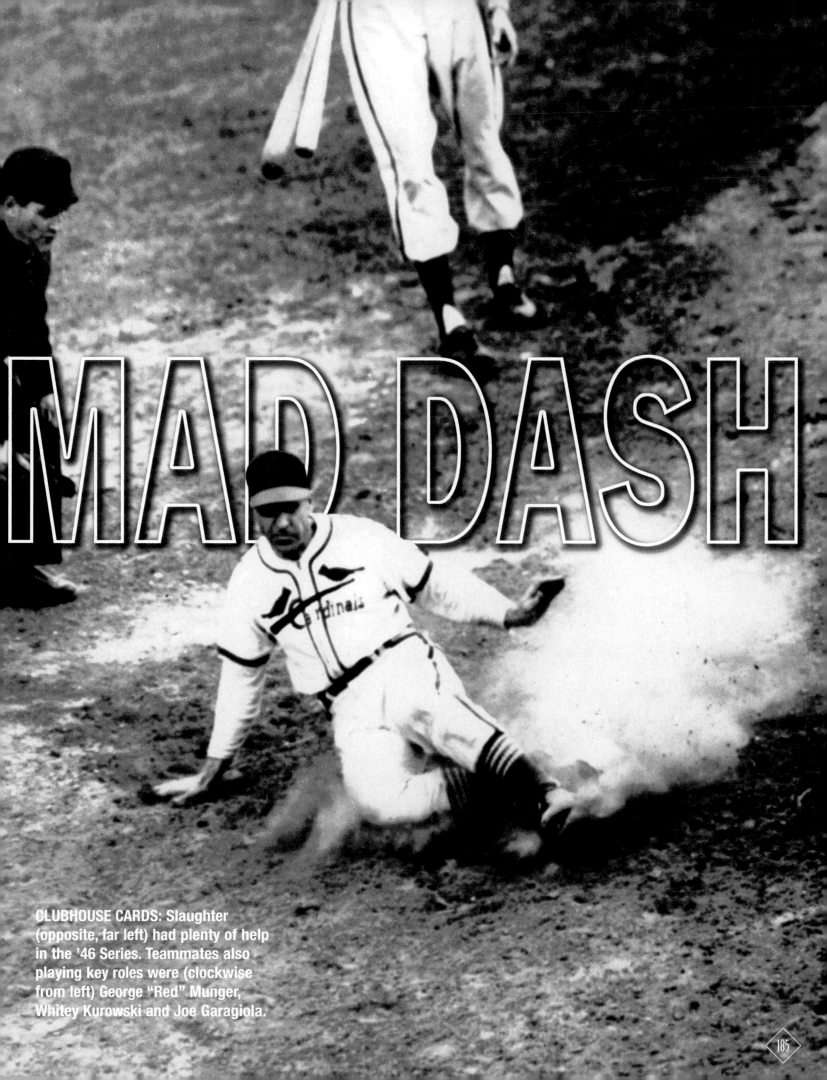

MAD DASH

CLUBHOUSE CARDS: Slaughter (opposite, far left) had plenty of help in the '46 Series. Teammates also playing key roles were (clockwise from left) George "Red" Munger, Whitey Kurowski and Joe Garagiola.

"GO CRAZY, FOLKS, GO CRAZY!"

As Ozzie Smith came to bat in the bottom of the ninth inning in Game 5 of the 1985 National League Championship Series against the Dodgers, a graphic flashed on the television screen. Smith, it noted, had never hit a home run batting lefthanded as a major leaguer. Not one in 2,967 at-bats. Shockingly, Smith then lined a pitch from Tom Niedenfuer over the right-field wall, giving the Cardinals a 3-2 victory and a three-games-to-two lead in the NLCS, moving St. Louis one win from a berth in the World Series.

"Smith corks one into right, down the line, it may go. ... Go crazy, folks, go crazy! It's a home run, and the Cardinals have won the game by the score of 3 to 2 on a home run by The Wizard. ... Go crazy!"

—Jack Buck

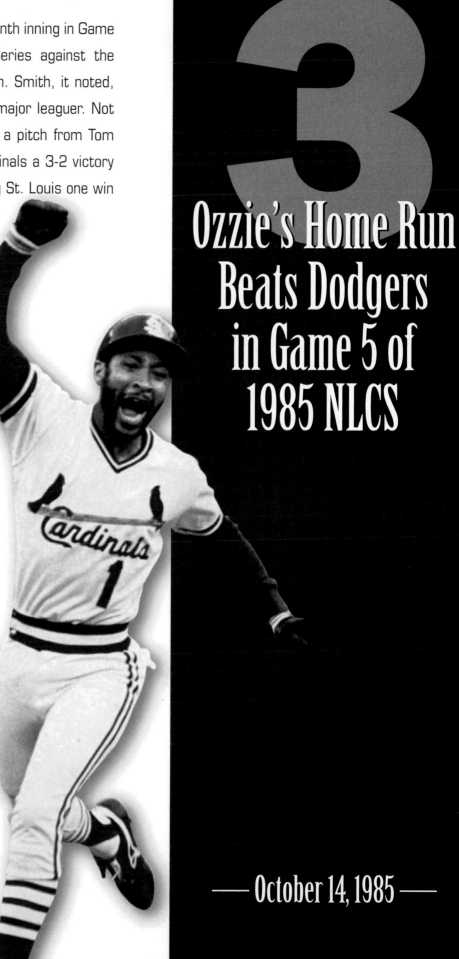

3

Ozzie's Home Run Beats Dodgers in Game 5 of 1985 NLCS

— October 14, 1985 —

When Bob Gibson struck out the Tigers' Al Kaline for the third time in the ninth inning of Game 1 of the 1968 World Series, it was the righthander's 15th strikeout of the day, tying the World Series record set by the Dodgers' Sandy Koufax in 1963. Gibson then shattered the mark by striking out Norm Cash, also for the third time, and he finished his breathtakingly dominant performance with strikeout No. 17, throwing a called third strike past Willie Horton. Dick McAuliffe (right) was Gibson's first strikeout victim of the game.

4

Gibson Strikes Out 17 in Game 1 of the 1968 World Series

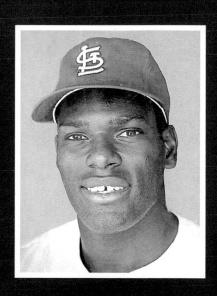

— October 2, 1968 —

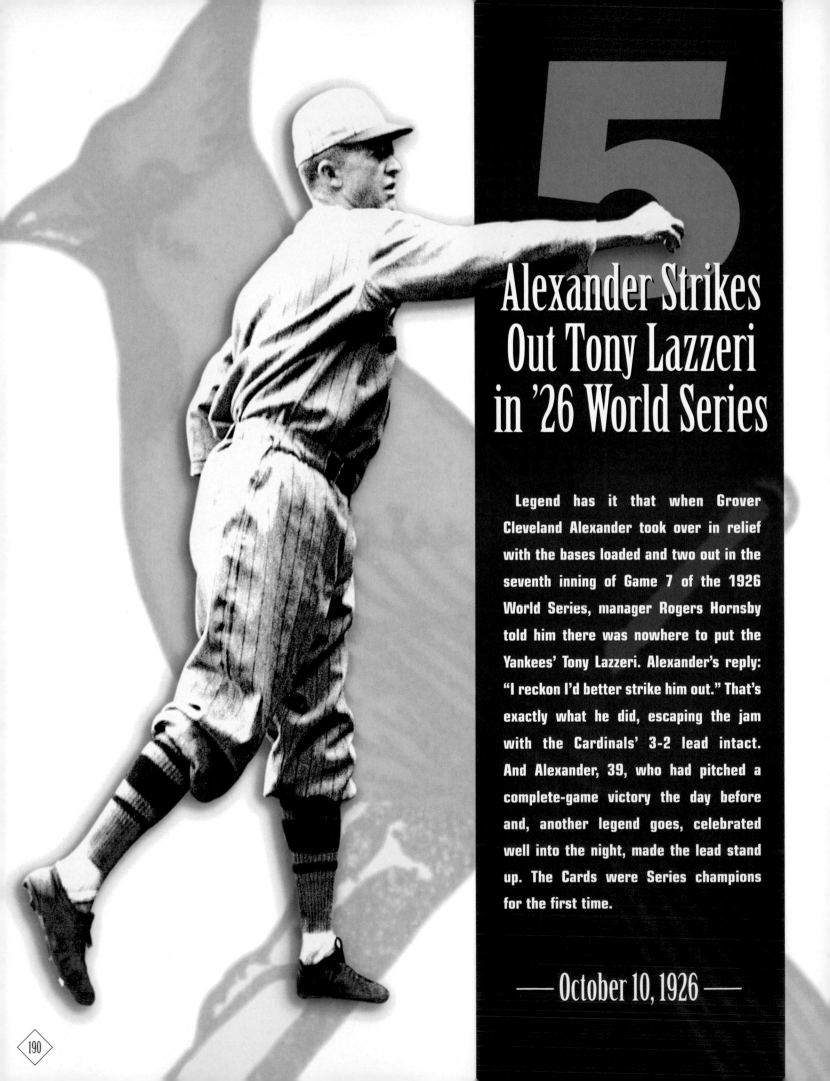

5

Alexander Strikes Out Tony Lazzeri in '26 World Series

Legend has it that when Grover Cleveland Alexander took over in relief with the bases loaded and two out in the seventh inning of Game 7 of the 1926 World Series, manager Rogers Hornsby told him there was nowhere to put the Yankees' Tony Lazzeri. Alexander's reply: "I reckon I'd better strike him out." That's exactly what he did, escaping the jam with the Cardinals' 3-2 lead intact. And Alexander, 39, who had pitched a complete-game victory the day before and, another legend goes, celebrated well into the night, made the lead stand up. The Cards were Series champions for the first time.

— October 10, 1926 —

> **" I reckon I'd better strike him out. "**

Game 6

Saturday, October 9, At New York

St. Louis	IP.	H.	R.	ER.	BB.	SO
Alexander (W)	9	8	2	2	2	6

Game 7

Sunday, October 10, At New York

St. Louis	IP.	H.	R.	ER.	BB.	SO
Haines (W)	6⅔	8	2	2	5	2
Alexander	2⅓	0	0	0	1	1

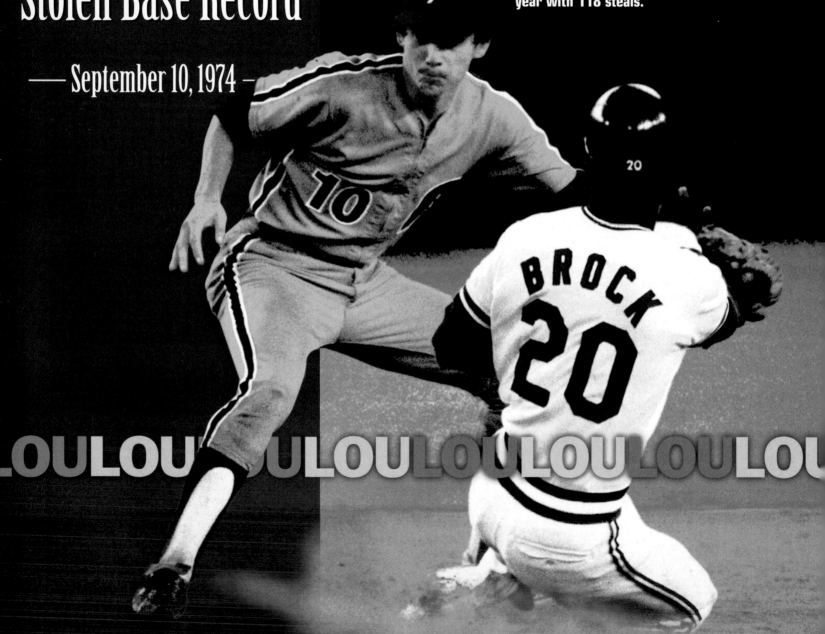

6

Lou Brock Breaks Maury Wills' Stolen Base Record

— September 10, 1974 —

Lou Brock had been the game's best basestealer long before the 1974 season, but he had never stolen more than 74 bases in one year. Running wild at age 35 in the summer of '74, Brock was in hot pursuit of Maury Wills' major league record of 104 stolen bases in one season—he had 60 steals by the All-Star break. In a September 10 game against the Phillies at Busch Stadium, Brock tied Wills' record in the first inning and broke it in the seventh. When Brock made history, Dick Ruthven was the Phils' pitcher, Bob Boone their catcher and Larry Bowa their shortstop (below, attempting the tag). Cool Papa Bell (opposite), known for his speed and basestealing prowess for St. Louis' old Negro leagues team, presented the base to Brock. Lou finished the year with 118 steals.

LOULOU

105

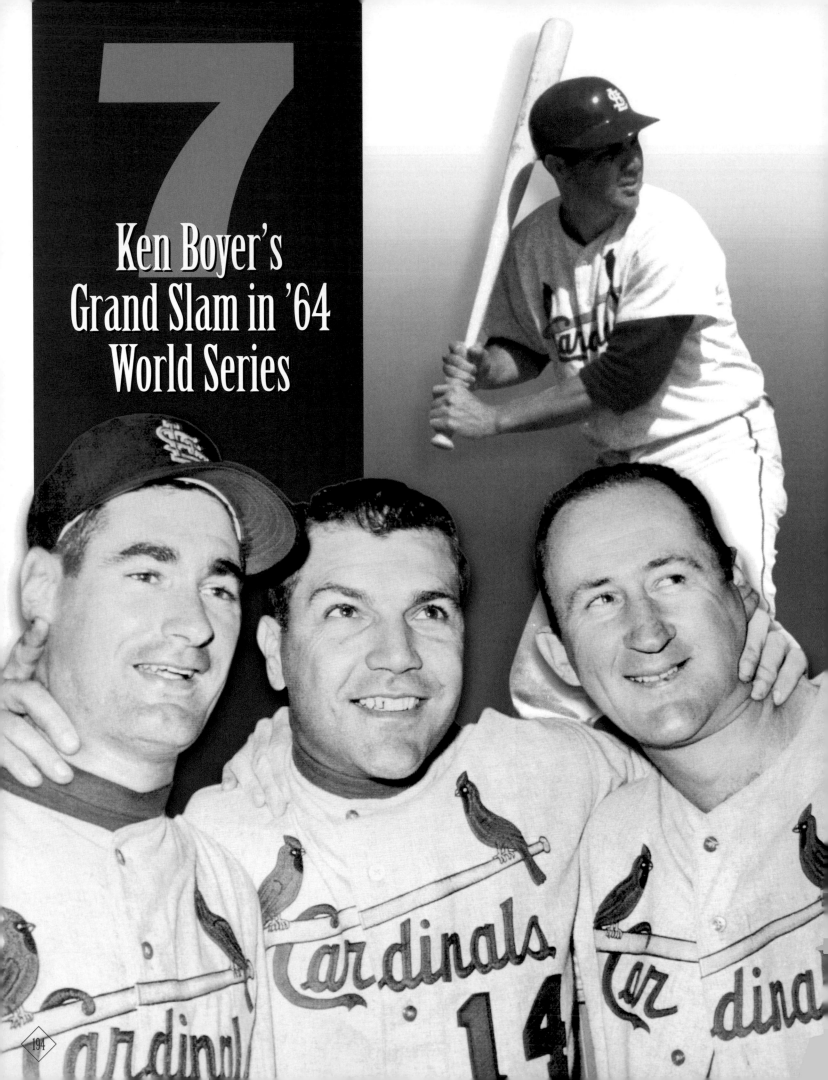

7

Ken Boyer's Grand Slam in '64 World Series

194

The Cardinals were facing a daunting task in the 1964 World Series. Down two games to one to the Yankees, they were trailing, 3-0, in the sixth inning of Game 4 at Yankee Stadium. Staring at the possibility of a three games-to-one deficit, the Cardinals filled the bases with one out against Al Downing. Ken Boyer, coming off what would be voted a Most Valuable Player season, came to the plate and rescued the Cards with a stadium-quieting grand slam. St. Louis held on to the 4-3 lead—the Cards got 8⅔ innings of scoreless relief that day from Roger Craig (opposite page, right) and Ron Taylor (opposite, far left)—and won the Series in seven games.

— October 11, 1964 —

GRAND SLAM

DECISIONS, DECISIONS: Dodgers manager Tommy Lasorda (2) made a bad one when he allowed Tom Niedenfuer (49) to face Jack Clark, who turned on the first pitch he saw (black and white photo, above).

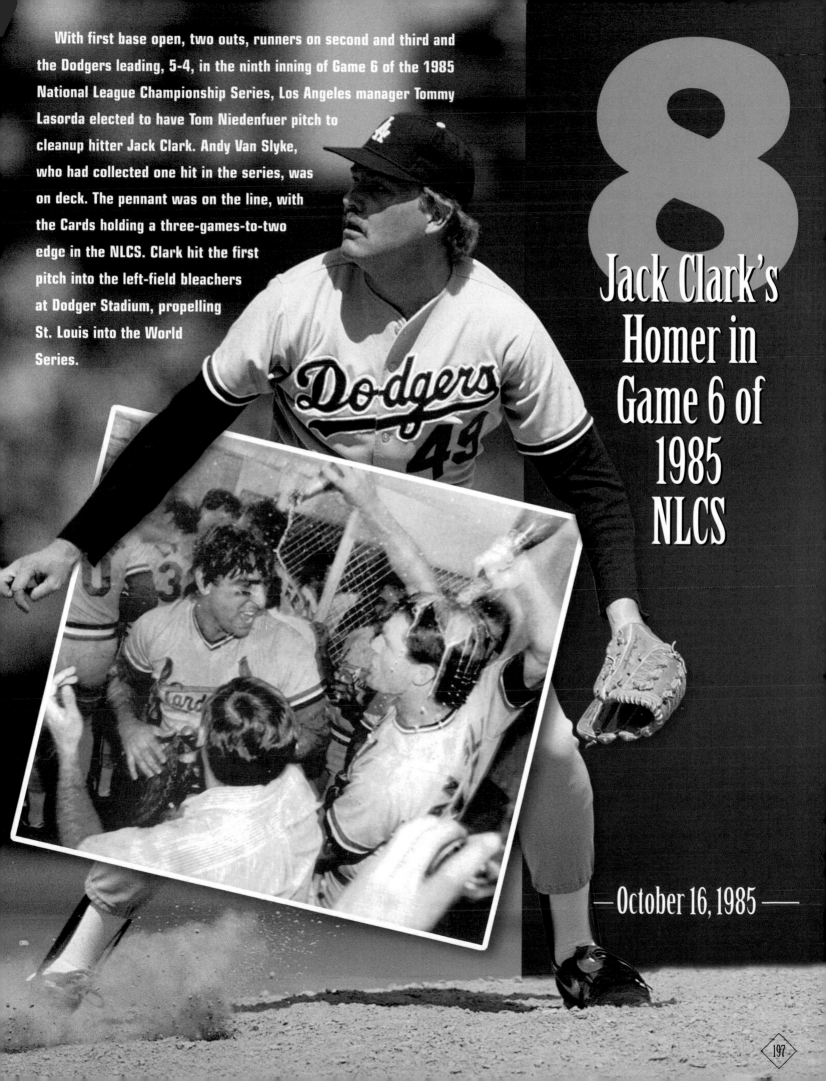

With first base open, two outs, runners on second and third and the Dodgers leading, 5-4, in the ninth inning of Game 6 of the 1985 National League Championship Series, Los Angeles manager Tommy Lasorda elected to have Tom Niedenfuer pitch to cleanup hitter Jack Clark. Andy Van Slyke, who had collected one hit in the series, was on deck. The pennant was on the line, with the Cards holding a three-games-to-two edge in the NLCS. Clark hit the first pitch into the left-field bleachers at Dodger Stadium, propelling St. Louis into the World Series.

8

Jack Clark's Homer in Game 6 of 1985 NLCS

— October 16, 1985 —

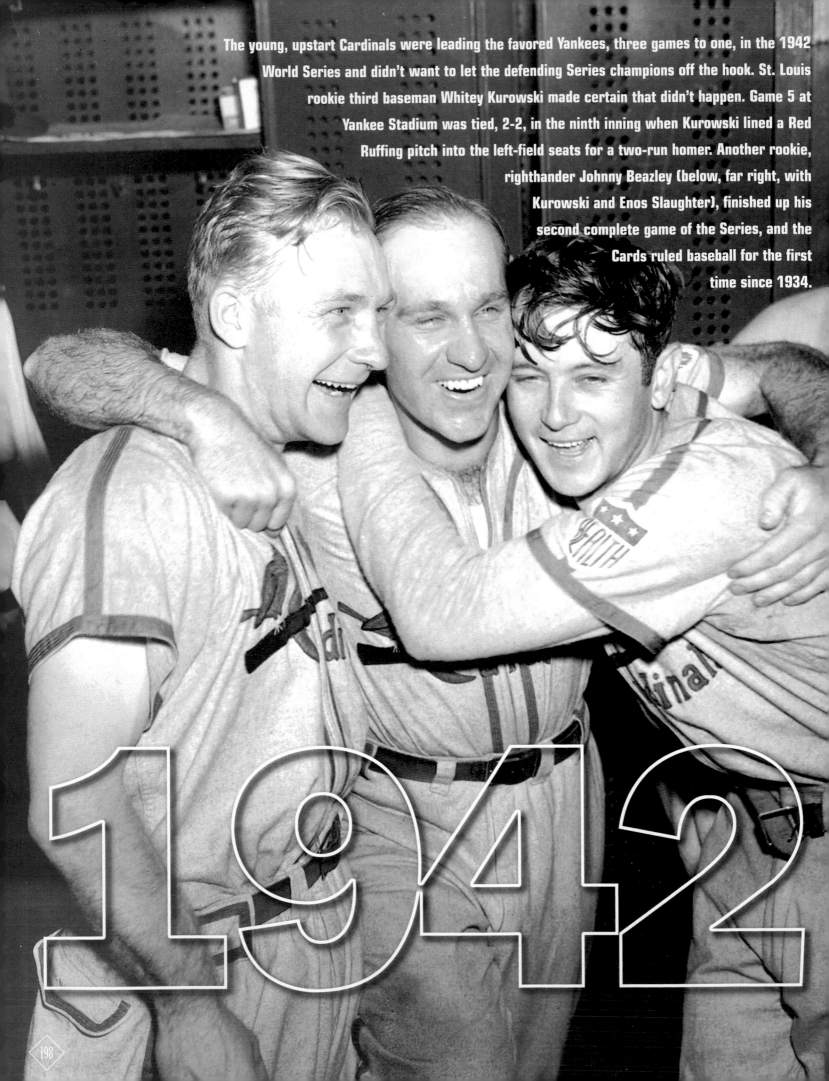

The young, upstart Cardinals were leading the favored Yankees, three games to one, in the 1942 World Series and didn't want to let the defending Series champions off the hook. St. Louis rookie third baseman Whitey Kurowski made certain that didn't happen. Game 5 at Yankee Stadium was tied, 2-2, in the ninth inning when Kurowski lined a Red Ruffing pitch into the left-field seats for a two-run homer. Another rookie, righthander Johnny Beazley (below, far right, with Kurowski and Enos Slaughter), finished up his second complete game of the Series, and the Cards ruled baseball for the first time since 1934.

1942

9

Kurowski's Home Run Wins '42 World Series

— October 5, 1942 —

10

Musial Collects 3,000th Hit

Cardinals manager Fred Hutchinson wanted Stan Musial to get his 3,000th career hit in St. Louis—so he left him out of the lineup for a May 13, 1958, game at Wrigley Field against the Cubs. Needing a pinch hitter in the sixth inning, though, Hutchinson called on Musial—and The Man came through with an RBI double off Moe Drabowsky for his milestone hit. Musial became only the eighth player in major league history to attain 3,000 hits.

— May 13, 1958 —

The GREATEST PERFORMANCES

BOB GIBSON

To call Bob Gibson's 1968 season the greatest performance in Cardinals history is not enough. His dazzling numbers add up to one of the finest years ever recorded by a pitcher in the game's history. Start with a minuscule earned-run average of 1.12, still a major league record for 300 or more innings pitched. Then consider a 22-9 won-lost record that featured 13 shutouts (the highest total in the majors since 1916)—and 28 complete games in 34 starts. Plus, Gibson struck out a league-high 268 batters and walked only 62 in 304⅓ innings.

After batting .397 in 1921 and .401 in 1922, Rogers Hornsby "slumped" to a .384 mark in 1923. The man acknowledged as the game's greatest righthanded hitter responded with an astonishing .424 average in 1924, a post-1900 major league high. He also led the league that year in runs scored (121), hits (227), doubles (43), walks (89) and slugging percentage (.696). The No. 2 man in the batting race wound up 49 points behind Hornsby, and the runner-up in slugging percentage finished at .552. Hornsby was amid a remarkable tear—from 1921 through 1925, he batted .402.

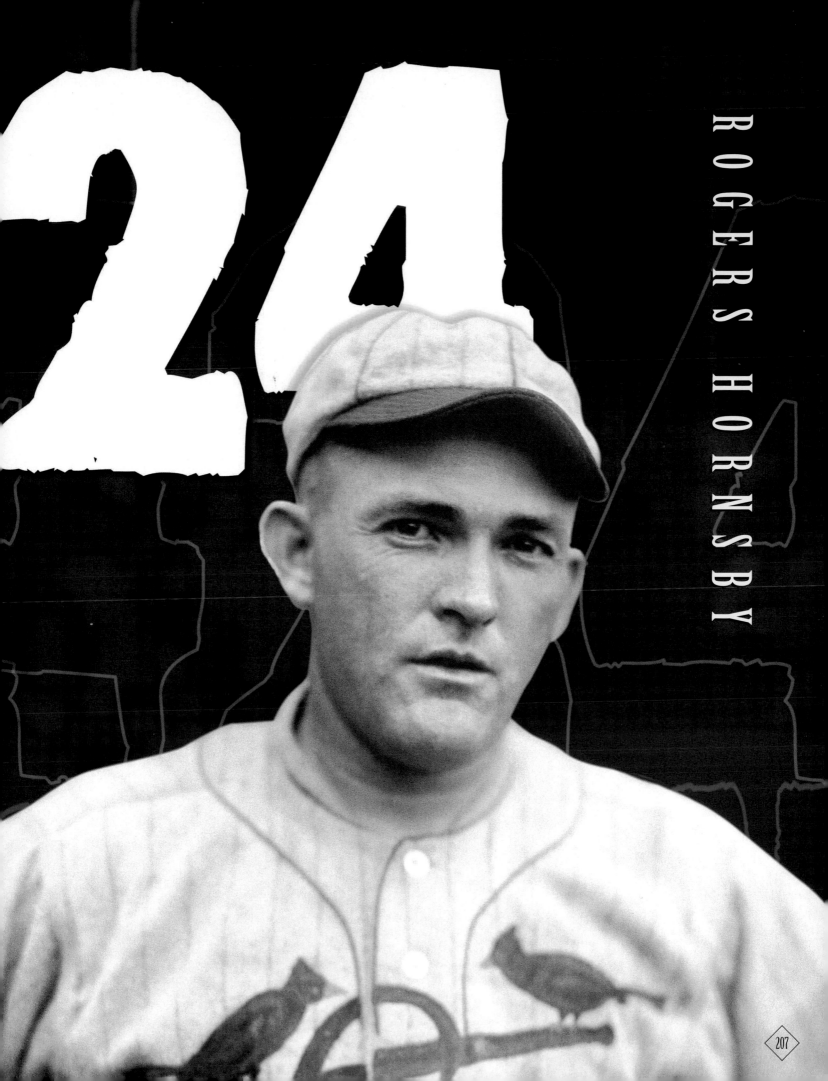

24

3

DIZZY DEAN

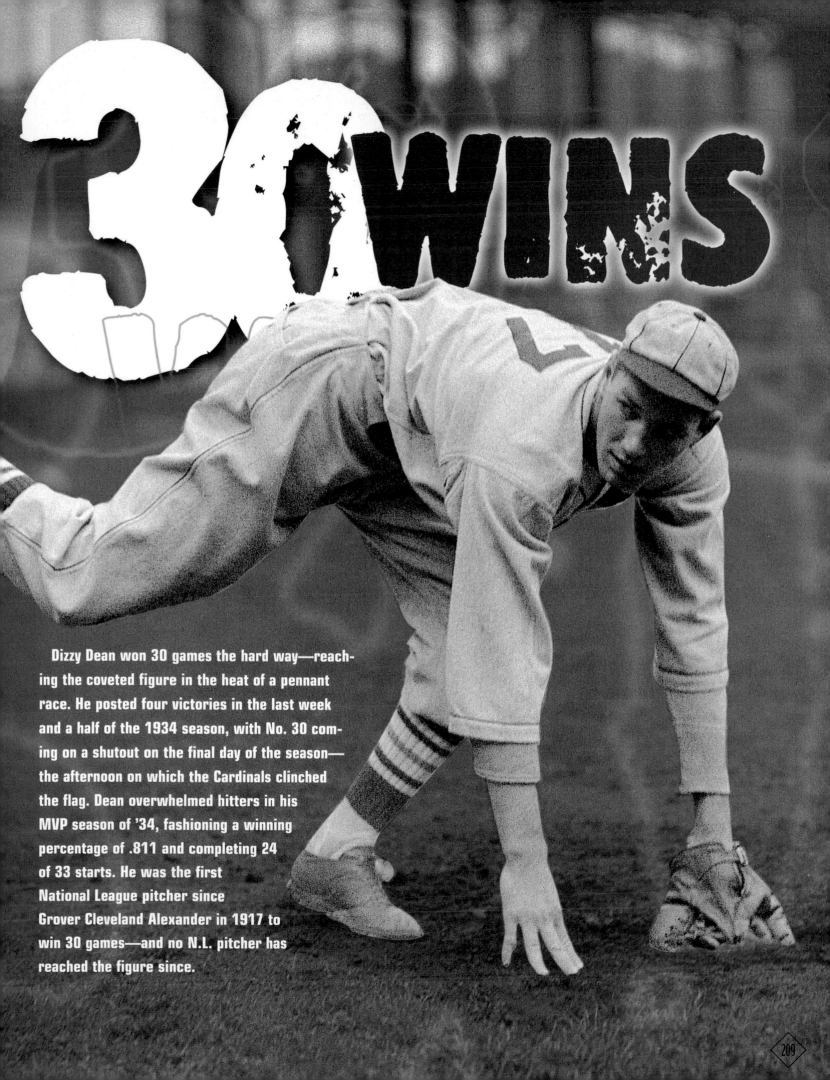

30 WINS

Dizzy Dean won 30 games the hard way—reaching the coveted figure in the heat of a pennant race. He posted four victories in the last week and a half of the 1934 season, with No. 30 coming on a shutout on the final day of the season—the afternoon on which the Cardinals clinched the flag. Dean overwhelmed hitters in his MVP season of '34, fashioning a winning percentage of .811 and completing 24 of 33 starts. He was the first National League pitcher since Grover Cleveland Alexander in 1917 to win 30 games—and no N.L. pitcher has reached the figure since.

Coming back from a broken leg is one thing. Coming back the way Bob Gibson did in the 1967 World Series is quite another. Sidelined eight weeks after being struck by a smash off the bat of Pittsburgh's Roberto Clemente in mid-July, Gibson rounded into shape with five starts in the final weeks of the regular season. He appeared primed for the Series against Boston (left, with Red Sox Game 1 starter Jose Santiago)— and that is an understatement. Gibson won the opener, 2-1, striking out 10 batters; he threw a five-hit shutout in Game 4; and in Game 7, he was a 7-2 winner, again fanned 10 and hit a home run. Three victories, three complete games, 14 hits allowed and a 1.00 ERA.

BOB GIBSON

SERIES

HOME RUNS IN A

On May 2, 1954, in St. Louis against the New York Giants, Stan Musial did what no one had ever done—he hit five home runs in a doubleheader. After connecting for three homers in the opener—two off Johnny Antonelli and one against Jim Hearn—Musial delivered an encore of two homers, both off Hoyt Wilhelm. He was retired on another long drive, a 410-foot smash that center fielder Willie Mays ran down in the nightcap. Musial was 4-for-4 in the first game and 6-for-8 overall, and he finished the day with nine RBIs. Somehow, the Cards managed only a split of the two games.

DOUBLEHEADER

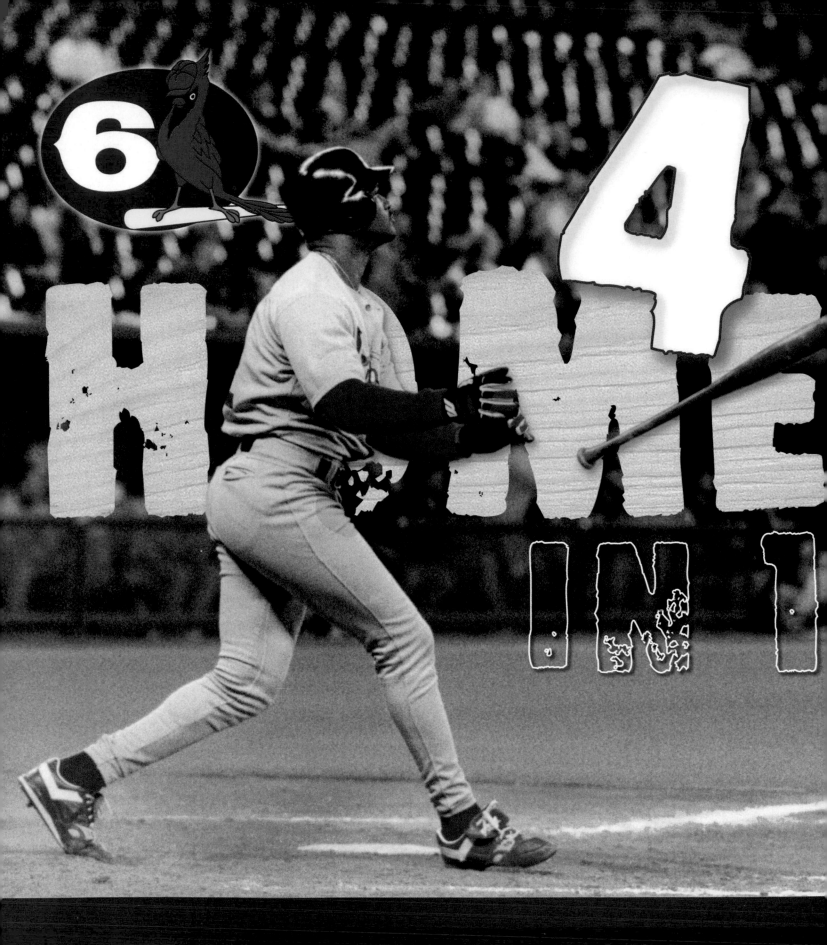

6

HOME 4 IN 1

Mark Whiten was playing in only his fourth major league season and had just 38 career home runs entering the Cardinals' September 7, 1993, doubleheader in Cincinnati. After going 0-for-4 with one RBI in the opener, Whiten went on an unfathomable spree in the second game. He became the 12th player in big-league history to hit four home runs in one game and only the second to drive in 12 runs in a single contest. He blasted a grand slam off Larry Luebbers in the first inning, three-run homers against Mike Anderson in the sixth and seventh and a two-run homer off Rob Dibble in the ninth.

MARK WHITEN

RUNS
GAME

JIM BOTTOMLEY

7

12 RBIs IN

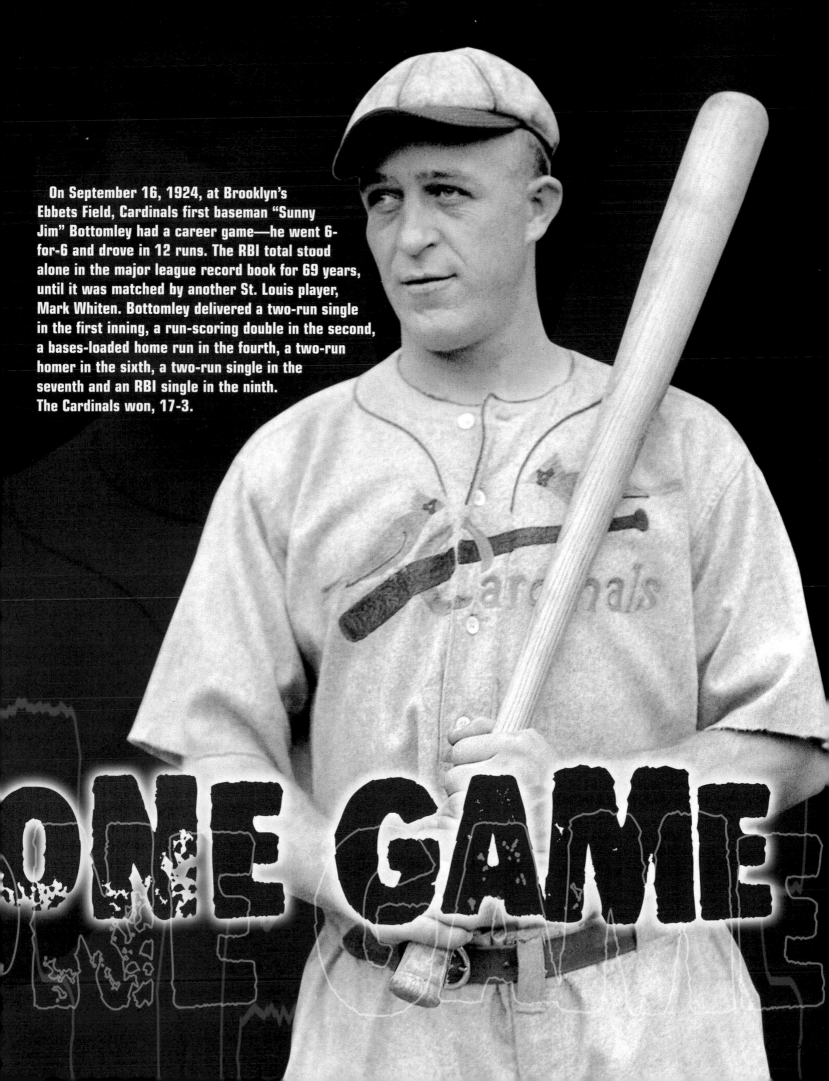

On September 16, 1924, at Brooklyn's Ebbets Field, Cardinals first baseman "Sunny Jim" Bottomley had a career game—he went 6-for-6 and drove in 12 runs. The RBI total stood alone in the major league record book for 69 years, until it was matched by another St. Louis player, Mark Whiten. Bottomley delivered a two-run single in the first inning, a run-scoring double in the second, a bases-loaded home run in the fourth, a two-run homer in the sixth, a two-run single in the seventh and an RBI single in the ninth. The Cardinals won, 17-3.

ONE GAME

8

PEPPER MARTIN

'31 WORLD SERIES

It was a dramatic way for Pepper Martin to cap his first season of full-time duty in the major leagues. Taking center stage in the Cardinals' seven-game World Series victory over the Philadelphia Athletics in 1931, center fielder Martin batted .500, drove in five runs, scored five times and stole five bases. The "Wild Horse of the Osage," who collected 12 hits in his first 18 at-bats in the '31 Series, went 3-for-4 in both Game 1 and Game 5 (a contest in which he hit a two-run homer off Waite Hoyt and knocked in four runs).

SHUTOUTS 5

Cardinals rookie lefthander Larry Jaster started five games against the National League champion Los Angeles Dodgers in 1966—and he shut out the Dodgers all five times. In an odd twist, Jaster spent six weeks in the minors between his first and second shutouts of Los Angeles. The Dodgers never even managed an extra-base hit off Jaster, who allowed 24 singles over 45 innings and spun his shutouts on April 25, July 3, July 29, August 19 and September 28. Jaster was 6-5 against the rest of the league with no shutouts. He wound up pitching four seasons with the Cards, going 32-25.

LARRY JASTER

GRAND
INNING

Major league baseball had been played for 123 seasons and no one had done what Cardinals third baseman Fernando Tatis accomplished at Dodger Stadium on the night of April 23, 1999—he cracked two grand slams in the same inning. Tatis' bases-full home runs came in the third inning off Los Angeles starter Chan Ho Park, the first coming with no one out and the second with two out. The magnitude of Tatis' feat was clear: His extraordinary night marked only the 10th time that a player had even hit two grand slams in one game. The Cards won, 12-5.

SLAMS

FERNANDO TATIS

The
CARDINALS
CHRONOLOGY

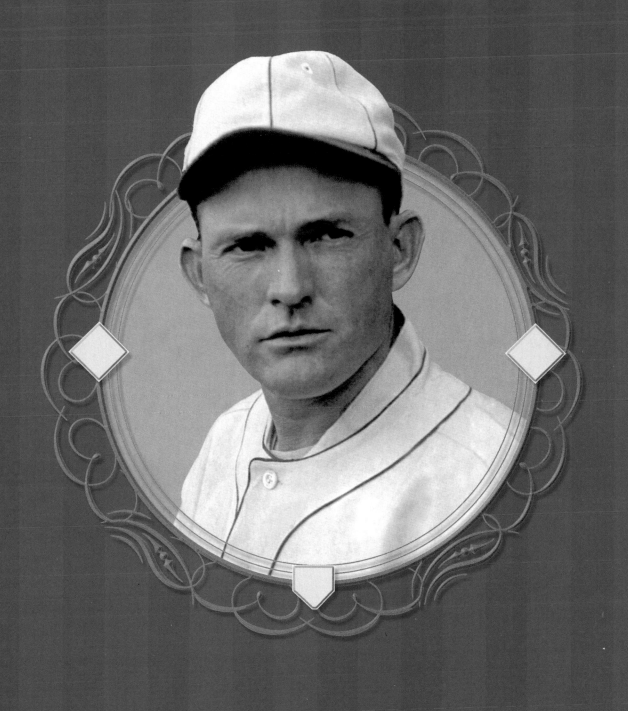

CARDINALS CHRONOLOGY

1892

Apr. 12—The Cardinals franchise—known first as the Browns, later as the Perfectos and then as the Cardinals—makes its National League debut with a 14-10 loss to the Chicago Colts at Sportsman's Park, located at Grand Avenue and Dodier Street. In later years, the Chicago franchise would be renamed the Cubs.

Apr. 17—The Browns lose, 5-1, to Cincinnati in the first National League game played on a Sunday. The club had played many Sunday games during its 10-year tenure in the American Association (a former "major league") and was allowed to keep the tradition as part of its agreement to enter the N.L.

Oct. 13—The Browns end their inaugural N.L. season. The season is split in half and the Browns perform poorly in each, going 31-42 in the first half and compiling a 25-52 record in the second. The overall record of 56-94 places them 11th in the 12-team league, 46 games behind the first-place Boston club. Five managers are employed by the Browns, and about the only bright spot for the team is righthanded pitcher Kid Gleason, who becomes the franchise's first 20-game winner (20-24).

1893

March 7—In an important rule change, the N.L. eliminates the pitching box and adds a pitcher's rubber five feet behind the previous back line of the box, establishing the modern pitching distance of 60 feet, six inches.

Apr. 27—The Browns open the season at their new ballpark, to be known as Robison Field, at the corner of Natural Bridge and Vandeventer avenues. They defeat the Louisville Colonels in the opener, 4-2.

Sept. 30—The Browns close out the season with a doubleheader sweep of league champion Boston, with rookie catcher Duff Cooley going 6-for-6 in the second game, a 16-4 St. Louis romp. The weather is terrible and the attendance is low, about 1,500. Between games of the doubleheader a ceremony is held at which Joe Quinn, Charlie Frank and Ted Breitenstein of the Browns are given medals by The Sporting News, a St. Louis-based weekly magazine, for finishing first, second and third in a TSN poll for the most popular baseball player in America. Quinn celebrates by collecting eight hits in the doubleheader, the first player to accomplish the feat. The Browns lead the league with a 4.06 ERA but finish in 10th place at 57-75 because they rank 11th in scoring and allow more than two unearned runs per game.

1894

May 10—The Browns slug six home runs in a game but lose at Cincinnati, 18-9. Shoddy fielding and suspect pitching doom St. Louis as the Reds parlay nine singles, a walk, a hit batsman and two errors to score 11 runs in one inning. Frank Shugart and St. Louis native Heinie Peitz hit two homers apiece for the Browns.

Sept. 30—The Browns sweep a doubleheader at home against Washington and finish in ninth place at 56-76, 35 games behind N.L. champion Baltimore. Roger Connor, who finishes the season in second place on the all-time home run list, finds triples to his liking this season, finishing with a team-high 25. Connor had been acquired from the New York Giants earlier in the season.

1895

June 1—Connor goes 6-for-6 and the Browns rap out a team-record 30 hits in a victory over the Giants.

June 3—Connor hits the 122nd homer of his career to pass Harry Stovey and become major league baseball's all-time home run leader. The homer, Connor's fourth of the season, accounts for the Browns' only two runs in a 5-2 loss to Brooklyn.

Aug. 16—Tommy Dowd becomes the first player in franchise history to hit for the cycle.

Sept. 28—Under four managers, one of them being team owner Chris **Von der Ahe**, the Browns go 39-92 and finish in 11th place, 48½ games behind pennant-inning Baltimore and just four ahead of last-place Louisville.

VON DER AHE

1896

Jan.—The Browns' best pitcher, **Breitenstein**, angers Von der Ahe by performing in a play called "The Derby Winner" in a Baltimore theater. The time Breitenstein spends on his acting career,

the Browns owner feels, could be better spent getting in shape for the upcoming season. Breitenstein disagrees and takes his case before the National Board of Arbitration, claiming the St. Louis club had not reserved him by the March 1 deadline. While Breitenstein holds out, Von der Ahe orders his ace lefty to report by April 1 "in proper condition to play ball." Breitenstein pitches the entire 1896 season in St. Louis (and accounts for 18 of the team's 40 wins) but is sold by a disgruntled Von der Ahe to the Cincinnati Reds for a reported $10,000 after the season. It will not be the last time a star pitcher for the franchise and a club owner have such a hearty disagreement.

Sept. 3—The Boston Beaneaters pulverize the Browns, 28-7, as Billy Hamilton, Jimmy Collins and Fred Tenney each collect five hits.

Sept. 26—The Browns finish the season 40-90, including a 13-43 mark on the road. They finish 50½ games behind first-place Baltimore and just 2½ ahead of last-place Louisville. Three St. Louis pitchers lose 24 or more games—Breitenstein (26), Bill Hart (29) and Red Donahue (24). Connor hits 11 homers in the next-to-last season of his major league career.

1897

May 23—With his team mired in last place and desperate for fans, Von der Ahe opens a "shoot the chutes" waterslide at his ballpark. The waterslide quickly becomes more popular than the team but is removed after the season.

Sept. 2—The Browns win a 10-inning game at Baltimore, 4-3, behind rookie pitcher Willie Sudhoff. It would be the team's final victory of the season.

Sept. 26—The visiting Cincinnati Reds sweep a doubleheader from the Browns by scores of 10-4 and 8-6. The outcome shocks no one as the Browns enter the twin bill riding a 16-game losing streak and a 21-game skein against the Reds, a team they last beat in 1895.

Oct. 3—The Browns end a miserable season that includes a team-record 18 straight defeats with a doubleheader split against Washington. In the first game, 45-year-old **Cap Anson** belts two homers against St. Louis in his final day as a major league player. The Browns become just the second major league team to lose 100 games, going 29-102 and finishing 63½ games out of first place, 23½ games behind 11th-place Louisville.

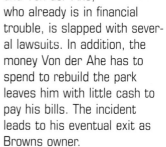

ANSON

1898

Apr. 16—During a game against the Chicago Orphans, a fire breaks out at the Browns' park and burns down most of the facility and Von der Ahe's saloon. Some 100 people are injured, several seriously, and Von der Ahe, who already is in financial trouble, is slapped with several lawsuits. In addition, the money Von der Ahe has to spend to rebuild the park leaves him with little cash to pay his bills. The incident leads to his eventual exit as Browns owner.

Apr. 17—After nearly 150 carpenters (and many Browns players) spend much of the previous night working at the burned-out ballpark to make it playable again, the Browns are clobbered by the Orphans, 14-1. The game is never in doubt as Chicago scores 10 runs in the fourth inning and the Browns, many weary from helping to rebuild a ballpark the night before, commit 11 errors. Typical is the play of Lou Bierbauer, who plays so poorly at second base that he is yanked by disgruntled first-year manager Tim Hurst, who doesn't seem to understand why his players are tired.

Oct. 15—The Browns finish 63½ games out of first place for the second consecutive season. At 39-111, St. Louis sets a major league record for losses.

1899

March 14—Von der Ahe's reign as Browns owner ends when the club, after some negotiations, is awarded April 3 to Frank de Haas Robison and **Matthew Stanley Robison**. The Robisons also own the Cleveland Spiders and move Cleveland's best players, including **Cy Young**, Jesse Burkett and Bobby Wallace, over to the Browns.

YOUNG

Apr. 15—St. Louis opens a season of considerable promise with a 10-1 romp over Cleveland. Red replaces brown as the coloring on the team's uniforms and the team nickname is now the Perfectos.

Aug. 1—With St. Louis and Boston tied, 7-7, in the 14th inning, Perfectos pitcher Jack Powell hits a ball over the head of center fielder Billy Hamilton for a game-winning, inside-the-park homer.

Oct. 15—A season that opened with much excitement ends with St. Louis posting its first winning season (84-67). Burkett becomes the first player in club history to have a 200-hit season (228). After the season, the Robisons take up a suggestion by sports reporter William McHale to rename the team the Cardinals.

1900

March 8—The N.L. shrinks from 12 to eight teams and players from the four eliminated teams (Baltimore, Cleveland, Louisville and Washington) are sold to the remaining clubs. The Cardinals purchase third baseman-manager **John McGraw**, catcher Wilbert Robinson and infielder Bill Keister from Brooklyn after McGraw and Robinson—who played for Baltimore in 1899—express their desire not to play for Brooklyn in 1900. The two former Baltimore stars, after a prolonged contract holdout, make their Cardinal debuts on May 12.

May 12—McGraw, leading off and playing third base, reaches base in four of his five at-bats and drives in a run in his first game with St. Louis. But he makes an error in the ninth inning that contributes to a 5-4 loss to the visiting Brooklyn Superbas, who score three runs in the final frame. For his part, Robinson goes 3-for-4 at the plate, including a ball that hits a flag pole on the left-field line and bounces back onto the field for a double.

Oct. 14—The Cardinals finish 65-75 and slip into a tie for fifth place, 19 games behind first-place Brooklyn. Young goes 20-18 in his final season with the club and allows a team-record 337 hits. McGraw, Robinson and Young leave the Cardinals at the end of the season to join Ban Johnson's newly formed American League.

1901

July 8—Pandemonium rules as St. Louis fans take umbrage at two calls by umpire Hank O'Day and nearly kill the arbiter following a 7-6 loss to Brooklyn. In the eighth inning, with the Cardinals leading, 4-3, O'Day calls two Brooklyn baserunners safe on the same play when they appear to be out. One of the runners, Cozy Dolan, runs five to 10 feet into the infield to avoid being tagged out after hitting a weak grounder to first baseman Dan McGann. By rule, he should have been out. The second runner, Tom Daly, appears clearly to be tagged out by Cardinals catcher Jack Ryan as he tries to score from third base. But both are ruled safe. The St. Louis players, faced with a one-out, two-on jam and a tie game instead of an inning-ending double play, argue vehemently with O'Day, but to no avail. Some fans toss beer bottles toward O'Day and others jump from the bleacher seats, hoping to get their hands on the beleaguered ump. When order is finally restored and the game is resumed, both runners eventually score to give the Superbas a 6-4 lead. Police have to escort O'Day from the field.

July 15—Giants rookie Christy Mathewson pitches a 5-0 no-hitter against the Cardinals in St. Louis.

Sept. 19—All games are canceled out of respect for the funeral of President William McKinley, which is held this day. McKinley, who is shot by an assassin on September 6, died on September 14.

Oct. 6—The Cardinals improve to 76-64 and finish fourth, 14½ games behind N.L. champion Pittsburgh. Burkett hits .376 to win his third and final batting title.

1902

May 6—The Robisons lose a lawsuit that attempts to block Burkett, Wallace and pitcher Jack Harper from joining St. Louis' American League club, the Browns.

June 3—Pitcher **Mike O'Neill** hits the first pinch-hit grand slam in major league history off Boston's Togie Pittinger in an 11-9 St. Louis triumph. It is an inside-the-park homer that scores his brother Jack.

Aug. 17—The Cardinals and Brooklyn Superbas play an 18-inning, 7-7 deadlock in a game called because of darkness. Rookie righthander Clarence "Cupid" Currie pitches 16 innings out of the bullpen for St. Louis.

Oct. 5—The Cardinals are swept at home in a double-header against Chicago and finish the season in sixth place at 56-78, 44½ games behind N.L. champ Pittsburgh.

O'NEILL

1903

July 22—The Cardinals win their fourth consecutive game in their final at-bat, this time 8-7 over Cincinnati. After the Reds score two runs in the top of the ninth to take a 7-5 lead, outfielder Homer Smoot swats a three-run homer with two out in the bottom of the inning to give St. Louis the victory. The Cardinals' starter is rookie righthander **Mordecai Brown**, a three-fingered Indiana coal miner who allows nine hits over four innings.

Sept. 27—The Cardinals split a season-ending doubleheader with Philadelphia and finish in last place at 43-94, 46½ games behind first-place Pittsburgh.

Dec. 12—The Cardinals trade Brown, coming off a 9-13 debut season, and catcher Jack O'Neill to the Cubs for catcher Larry McLean and pitcher Jack Taylor. It's a terrible trade for the Cardinals, as Brown will go on to a Hall of Fame career with Chicago, including six straight 20-win seasons (1906-11).

1904

Feb. 1—The Cardinals purchase veteran first baseman Jake Beckley from the Cincinnati Reds. Beckley, who has 2,501 career hits, will add just 429 to that total in his final four big-league seasons in St. Louis.

June 16—Mathewson, a loser against St. Louis on May 4, beats the Cardinals for the first of six times this season and what will become 24 straight times overall. Of course, Mathewson beats more teams than just St. Louis in 1904—the Giants' star righthander goes 33-12 and leads the league in strikeouts.

Oct. 4—Taylor pitches his 39th consecutive complete game, a N.L. single-season record. It comes one day after Mathewson strikes out a record 16 Cardinals in a 3-1 Giants victory.

Oct. 9—The Cardinals improve by 32 victories in the first season of the 154-game schedule but finish in fifth place at 75-79, 31½ games behind the pennant-winning New York Giants.

1905

Feb. 15—Taylor, who was accused of throwing games by Cubs owner James Hart, is acquitted by the league office but fined $300 for bad conduct.

May 29—Six days before he is traded to Pittsburgh, Cardinals infielder Dave Brain hits three triples in a game against his future Pirate teammates.

Oct. 8—The Cardinals lose both ends of a doubleheader at Chicago and finish in sixth place at 58-96, 47½ games behind the first-place Giants.

Oct. 15—The Browns sweep a doubleheader against the Cardinals to win the "City Series." The scores are 7-6 and 3-0, with the second game being called because of darkness after six innings. Harry Howell wins both games for the Browns while Taylor loses both for the Cardinals. Future Hall of Famer Bill Klem umpires both games, which are played one day after the end of a five-game World Series between the New York Giants and Philadelphia Athletics.

1906

Apr. 28—The Pirates beat the Cardinals, 10-1, a game highlighted by a steal of home by Pittsburgh player-manager Fred Clarke.

June 9—The N.L.'s worst team, the Boston Beaneaters, snap a 19-game losing streak by defeating the Cardinals.

July 20—Brooklyn's Mal Eason no-hits the Cardinals.

August 13—Taylor, after being traded to the Cubs on July 1, is knocked out in the third inning of a game against Brooklyn, ending a string of 187 complete games and 15 relief appearances in which he finishes each game. The streak began in 1901 during Taylor's first stint with the Cubs.

Oct. 7—The Cardinals finish in seventh place at 52-98, 63 games behind first-place Chicago and just 2½ games ahead of last-place Boston. No St. Louis pitcher wins more than nine games and Beckley leads the team with 44 RBIs. As a team, the Cardinals hit a franchise-low 10 home runs.

1907

May 20—The Cardinals beat the Giants, 6-4, at the Polo Grounds to end New York's 17-game winning streak.

Aug. 11—The Cardinals complete a five-game sweep of Boston by winning two games in St. Louis, 5-4 and 4-0. A crowd of 12,000—the largest of the season—looks on as righthander Stoney McGlynn and lefty Ed Karger befuddle the Boston batsmen. In the second game, which is limited to seven innings by mutual agreement of the teams, Karger does not allow a hit. He is so dominant that had the game lasted the normal nine innings, Karger likely would have pitched the only perfect game in Cardinals history.

Sept. 1—The Cardinals rally from a 2-0, ninth-inning deficit at Chicago by scoring seven runs against Cubs righthander Ed Reulbach for a 7-2 win. What makes the victory so stunning is that the Cardinals are a last-place team while Reulbach is a star who will finish the season with a 17-4 record and 1.69 ERA.

Sept. 30—The Cardinals set a major league record with three steals of home in a game against Boston. Ed Konetchy performs the feat twice and fellow rookie Joe Delahanty, younger brother of Hall of Famer Ed, does it once.

Oct. 6—The Cardinals split a doubleheader at home against the Cubs and finish in last place at 52-101. The Cardinals hit just .232 for the season and McGlynn loses a team-record 25 games.

1908

Apr. 20—Despite allowing just one hit—and a disputed one at that—to the visiting Chicago Cubs, Cardinals righthander Bugs Raymond loses his first start of the season, 2-0. Raymond's teammates offer him little support, getting six hits off Cubs starter Carl Lundgren and committing five errors in the field. It would have been six had a grounder by Harry Steinfeldt that went through the legs of shortstop Patsy O'Rourke—the only "hit" he allows—been ruled correctly.

BRESNAHAN

Sept. 15—**Mathewson** beats the Cardinals for the 24th consecutive time, setting a record for dominance against an opponent.

Sept. 25—Frank de Haas Robison dies of a stroke at age 54 in Cleveland.

Oct. 4—A miserable season ends with a 5-1 loss at Cincinnati. The Cardinals, who lose a team-record 27 games in September, drop into the N.L. cellar at 49-105 and finish 50 games behind the first-place Cubs. St. Louis is shut out 33 times and commits 93 more errors than the league's next-worst fielding team. Raymond loses 25 games, 11 by shutout.

Dec. 12—The Cardinals acquire catcher **Roger Bresnahan** from the Giants for three players and give him a four-year deal to be a player-manager.

1909

May 24—After 24 straight losses to Mathewson, the Cardinals finally beat the future Hall of Famer, 3-1 in New York. Mathewson isn't bad, but Cardinals lefty Johnny Lush is at least his equal and the Giants' fielders are terrible. All three St. Louis runs are unearned. The game is Bresnahan's first in New York after last December's trade.

July 3—The Cardinals are swept in a doubleheader at Cincinnati and tie a major league record as 17 players commit errors.

July 24—Brooklyn lefthander George "Nap" Rucker strikes out 16 Cardinals in a 1-0 win.

Aug. 4—Former Cardinals manager Tim Hurst, now an A.L. umpire, has to be escorted out of Philadelphia's Shibe Park under police protection following an altercation with A's star Eddie Collins. Hurst spits in Collins' face after calling him out on strikes. A.L. president Ban Johnson fires Hurst.

Oct. 6—The Cardinals go 54-98 in their first season under Bresnahan and finish seventh, 56 games behind first-place Pittsburgh. Fred Beebe, 15-21, becomes the team's fourth 20-game loser in five years.

1910

May 4—**William Howard Taft**, who in April had become the first U.S. president to throw out the ceremonial first pitch on opening day, takes in a Cardinals game in St. Louis. After seeing the Cardinals jump to a 12-3 lead against the Reds, he heads to Sportsman's Park to see the Browns and Cleveland Indians. The Browns and Indians please the president by locking up in a 3-3 duel that is called after 14 innings because of darkness.

June 1—Second baseman Miller Huggins comes to the plate six times in a game and doesn't record an official at-bat, finishing the day with four walks, a sacrifice hit and a sacrifice fly. Huggins winds up leading the N.L. with 116 walks.

Aug. 3—For the first time since 1901, Bresnahan pitches in a game, giving up six hits and no runs in 3⅓ innings against Brooklyn.

Oct. 15—The Cardinals end the season with a 4-1 road loss to the Cubs and finish seventh at 63-90, 40½ games behind first-place Chicago. Konetchy becomes the team's first .300 hitter in five years.

1911

Mar. 24—Cardinals owner Matthew Stanley Robison dies of heart attack in Cleveland. His niece, **Mrs. Helene Hathaway Robison Britton**, inherits the team and becomes the first female owner of a major league franchise.

May 13—In a 19-5 victory over the Cardinals, the Giants score 13 runs in the first inning, including a major league record 10 before the first out is made.

July 11—While his team is traveling by train from Washington to Boston, Bresnahan asks that their Pullman car be repositioned to the back of the train because it is too close to the noisy engine. The request is granted and shortly afterward, the train crashes down an 18-foot embankment just west of Bridgeport, Conn. The coach car that replaced the Cardinals' Pullman is destroyed and 14 people are killed. The Cardinal players help remove bodies and rescue the injured, then board another train to Boston, where the day's game is postponed.

Sept. 24—The Cardinals push across a run in the sixth inning of a game against Philadelphia to snap a string of 41 consecutive scoreless innings by rookie righthander Grover Cleveland Alexander.

Oct. 9—At 75-74, the Cardinals finish with a winning record for the first time since 1901. The record nets them a fifth-place finish, 22 games behind first-place New York.

1912

July 18—Konetchy has a streak of consecutive chances handled without an error end at 592 when he makes a poor throw in a game against Brooklyn.

Oct. 6—The Cardinals finish in sixth place at 63-90, 41 games behind first-place New York. One of the positives is the performance of pitcher Harry "Slim" Sallee, who goes 16-17 and leads the N.L. with six saves. The lanky left-hander's success comes despite the fact he is an insomniac who likes to stay up late at night to help milkmen make their rounds.

Oct. 22—With four years left on a contract that pays him $10,000 per season, Bresnahan, never a favorite of Mrs. Britton, is fired as manager and replaced by second baseman **Huggins**. Bresnahan insists the Cardinals honor his contract and the dispute is settled the following year, when Bresnahan is traded to the Cubs for cash.

1913

May 4—The Cardinals beat the Cubs, 10-8, in a 13-inning game at Chicago's West Side Park. Rookie manager Huggins, after using up all of his pitchers, relies on position players. His first choice, rookie outfielder Ted Cather, is hit hard and has to be replaced. His second choice, first baseman Konetchy, pitches 4⅔ innings to earn the only win of his big-league career.

June 5—Former team owner Chris Von der Ahe dies in St. Louis. According to legend, Von der Ahe had the year of his death inscribed on his life-sized, gravesite marker years before he died. Others contend that the story is false, yet another self-aggrandizing creation from the fertile mind of the late, unlamented owner.

Oct. 5—The Cardinals win their season finale in Cincinnati 4-1 to avoid the 100-loss mark. At 51-99, the Cardinals finish in last place, 49 games behind the first-place Giants.

1914

July 1—Righthander Casey Hageman pitches a 5-1 complete-game victory over Pittsburgh. Until the Pirates score their only run in the ninth inning, just two runners get as far as second base against the 27-year-old pitcher.

Aug. 26—More than 27,000 fans cram into Robison Field, which seats 17,000, to watch a doubleheader between the Cardinals and Giants, who are battling for the N.L. pennant. The Cardinals win the opener, 1-0, but are shut out by Mathewson in the second game, 4-0.

Oct. 5—A seven-game losing streak in September obliterates the Cardinals' chances of capturing their first N.L. pennant. At 81-72, St. Louis finishes in third place—its best finish since joining the N.L. A pitching staff that had allowed the most runs in the league the year before ties for the fewest allowed this year. Bill Doak leads the N.L. with a 1.72 ERA.

1915

Apr. 19—Pitcher Lee Meadows makes his major league debut, becoming the first player to wear eyeglasses regularly in the majors since 1886. Cardinals teammates call him Specs.

Aug. 30—The Cardinals, who lead, 2-0, after six innings, lose a heartbreaker at Philadelphia, 4-3, when a ball hit by Phillies outfielder George "Possum" Whitted in the bottom of the 10th inning bounces off the wall, then off the chest of Cardinals left fielder Bob Bescher and over the wall for a bizarre game-ending home run. The Phillies' starting pitcher in the game is Alexander, who goes on to lead the N.L. in wins, ERA, complete games, strikeouts and shutouts.

Sept. 10—Rogers Hornsby makes his big-league debut, replacing Artie Butler at shortstop in the seventh inning against the Reds. Hornsby goes 0-for-2 and makes his first start four days later.

Oct. 3—The Cardinals slip to sixth place at 72-81, 18½ games behind the first-place Phillies.

1916

May 14—Hornsby hits his first major league homer off Brooklyn righthander Jeff Pfeffer in a 3-2 loss at Robison Field. It is an inside-the-park homer for Hornsby, who will hit another 300 home runs in his career.

Oct. 1—The Cardinals end the season with a 6-3 loss to the Cubs at Chicago's Weeghman Park and tie the Reds for last place at 60-93. St. Louis collapses down the stretch, losing 28 of its final 33 games, including the last 14 (all on the road). The Cardinals score the fewest number of runs in the league and allow the most. An incensed club president Schuyler Britton, husband of club owner Helene Hathaway Robison Britton, promises "a thorough housecleaning" before the start of the 1917 season.

Oct.—Schuyler Britton's prediction eventually comes true, but he has little to do with it. Helene Britton sells the Cardinals to the team's attorney, James Jones. One of Jones' first moves changes the future of the franchise—he hires Branch Rickey away from his job as business manager of the St. Louis Browns to become the Cardinals' team president.

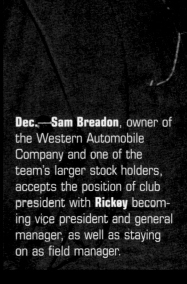

1917

June 11—Mike Gonzalez ends a pitching duel between Bill Doak of the Cardinals and Joe Oeschger of the Phillies by stealing home with two outs in the 15th inning to give St. Louis a thrilling 5-4 victory at Robison Field. After yielding four runs in the first inning, Doak holds the Phils scoreless over the next 14 frames.

Sept. 18—Doak pitches two complete-game victories on the same day (2-0 and 12-4).

Sept. 30—The Cardinals make a big turnaround and go 82-70 to finish third in the N.L. Hornsby hits .327 (second in the league) and leads the N.L. in triples, slugging and total bases.

Oct. 26—Huggins, disappointed with the team's new ownership, leaves the Cardinals to accept a two-year offer to manage the New York Yankees, a franchise he will lead to six pennants and three World Series titles from 1918 to 1929. The Cardinals subsequently sign minor league manager Jack Hendricks to manage the team in 1918.

1918

July 3—The old hidden-ball trick works to perfection as the last-place Cardinals defeat the first-place Cubs at Robison Field, 2-1. With Cub runners on second and third with one out in the ninth, St. Louis second baseman Bobby Fisher tricks the runner on second, Dode Paskert, into believing that he has handed the ball back to pitcher Red Ames after a conference on the mound with shortstop Hornsby. He hadn't, and after returning to his position Fisher tags the unaware Paskert as he ambles off the second-base bag. Ames then strikes out the next batter to preserve the win.

Aug. 26—Hornsby is thrown out of a game against the Giants and fined $50 by Hendricks. The two trade verbal jabs through the press until Rickey steps in and tells them to settle their differences in private.

Sept. 2—The season is cut short because of World War I, and the team finishes in last place at 51-78.

1919

Jan.—Rickey begins to lay the groundwork for his idea of a team-owned minor league farm system when he purchases a share of the Houston club of the Texas League. Rickey and the Cardinals will purchase other minor league teams as a way to develop and keep talent.

Jan. 26—The Cardinals announce Rickey will replace Hendricks as manager while continuing to serve as team president. One reason for the move is that the club finished last under Hendricks the year before. Another, as Rickey would later claim, is to save the team a manager's salary.

Sept. 28—The Cardinals finish seventh at 54-83, 40½ games behind N.L. champion Cincinnati. Hornsby, who plays in every game, misses the batting title by three points.

Oct. 12—Rickey holds the first of his annual tryout camps for anyone interested in pursuing a career as a professional baseball player. Among those signed to contracts are first baseman **Jim Bottomley** and outfielder **Ray Blades**.

Dec.—**Sam Breadon**, owner of the Western Automobile Company and one of the team's larger stock holders, accepts the position of club president with **Rickey** becoming vice president and general manager, as well as staying on as field manager.

BOTTOMLEY

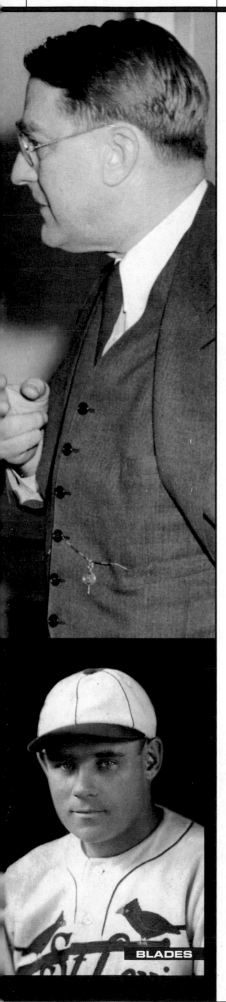

BLADES

1920

Jan.—The Cardinals borrow $10,000 to purchase minor leaguer Jesse Haines from Kansas City. Haines had compiled a 21-5 record at Kansas City in 1919 and fashioned a 2.11 ERA. The righthander, who pitched in one game with the Cincinnati Reds in 1918, will go on to pitch 18 seasons for the Cardinals, the most of any pitcher in team history.

June 6—Breadon sells Robison Field to the St. Louis school board for $275,000 and leases the use of Sportsman's Park from Browns owner Phil Ball for $35,000 per season. He also agrees to pay half of the annual cleanup cost at the ballpark.

July 1—The Cardinals move into Sportsman's Park—their home for the next 46 seasons—with a 6-2, 10-inning loss to the Pirates. This Sportsman's Park is located at the same site as Von der Ahe's first Sportsman's Park facility—on the west side of Grand between Dodier and Sullivan.

Sept. 17—The Cardinals set a major league record with 12 consecutive hits in a 9-4 victory over Boston.

Oct. 3—The Cardinals finish the season in a fifth-place dead-lock with the Cubs at 75-79. Hornsby hits .370 to win the first of six consecutive batting championships. He leads the league in doubles with 44 and in runs batted in with 94. Bill Doak wins 20 games; Haines loses 20.

1921

June 13—The Cardinals beat the Giants, 10-1, at Sportsman's Park for their club-record 10th straight victory. Center fielder Les Mann hits two home runs in support of Haines, who goes the distance for his sixth win in a row. The only negative comes in the eighth inning, when Hornsby hits into a bizarre 4-3-6 triple play.

Aug. 5—Harold Arlin is behind the microphone as the first radio broadcast of a major league game is heard over KDKA in Pittsburgh. The Pirates beat the Phillies, 8-5.

Oct. 2—The Cardinals end the season at 87-66, their highest win total since joining the N.L. They win 30 of their last 37 games to finish third, seven games behind first-place New York. Hornsby leads the league in runs, hits, doubles, RBIs and batting average. Promising young outfielder Austin McHenry hits .350, 47 points behind The Rajah but third in the league.

1922

Feb. 23—The Cardinals are hit by stunning news: catcher William "Pickles" Dillhoefer, a solid but unspectacular backup, is dead of pneumonia at age 27.

July 20—**Hornsby** sets a modern N.L. record with his 25th homer—a two-out, three-run shot in the bottom of the ninth to beat the Braves 7-6.

Aug. 18—Bottomley makes his major league debut.

Sept. 20—Hornsby's 33-game hitting streak, the longest in franchise history, ends against Brooklyn's Burleigh Grimes in the first game of a doubleheader at Ebbets Field.

Sept. 24—Hornsby hits his final two homers of the season—Nos. 41 and 42—in a 10-6 victory over the Giants in New York.

Oct. 1—Hornsby sets an N.L. record with 250 hits and also leads the league in homers and RBIs (152) to win the Triple Crown. The Cardinals finish in a tie for third place at 85-69.

Nov. 27—Two months after his 27th birthday, McHenry dies of a brain tumor at his Ohio home. The tumor had been discovered earlier in the season after McHenry, who had been complaining of headaches and having trouble judging fly balls in the outfield, was taken to a doctor by Rickey to get an examination.

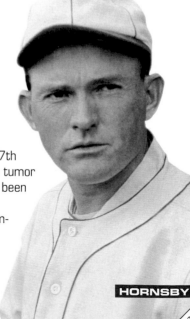

HORNSBY

1923

July 10—Rookie Johnny Stuart pitches two complete-game victories at Braves Field in Boston (11-1 and 6-3). They are the first starts of the season and just the second and third in the career of Stuart, a former football player at Ohio State.

Aug. 12—Hornsby curses out Rickey in the visitors clubhouse at the Polo Grounds in New York in a disagreement over strategy. According to accounts, coach Burt Shotton has to step in to keep the two apart. Rickey, his club muddling through a mediocre season, says the incident "amounted to nothing." Later in the season, Hornsby is suspended for five games after saying he is too ill to play while the team's doctors pronounce him fit.

Oct. 7—The Cardinals split a doubleheader at home against the Cubs and finish in fifth place at 79-74. Hornsby wins the batting title with a .384 average despite playing in only 107 games. Bottomley hits .371 in his first full big-league season.

1924

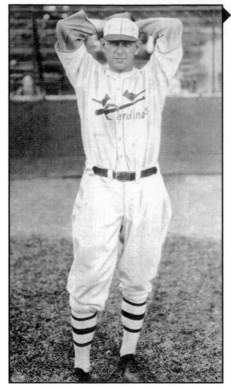

July 17—Haines pitches a 5-0 no-hitter against Boston at Sportsman's Park to become the first Cardinal to hurl a no-hitter.

July 19—Two days after Haines' feat, Herman Bell pitches two complete-game victories on the same day (6-1 and 2-1), allowing just six hits in the two games. The rookie, however, wins only one other game all season.

Sept. 16—In a 17-3 victory at Brooklyn, Bottomley sets a major league record with 12 RBIs in one game. His hits include three singles, a double and two homers. It is the first of two 6-for-6 games in the big-league career of the slugging first baseman, who breaks the RBI record of Brooklyn manager Wilbert Robinson.

Sept. 28—The Cardinals finish the season 65-89 and tumble to sixth place. Hornsby hits .424—the highest average ever in the 20th century—but doesn't win the N.L. MVP Award when a Cincinnati writer leaves Hornsby off his ballot.

1925

Apr. 22—The Cardinals score 11 runs in the first inning of their home opener in a 12-3 win over Cincinnati. The Cards pounce on Reds starter Pete Donohue, who had shut them out a week earlier in Cincinnati.

May 30—On Memorial Day, with his team sporting a 13-25 record, Breadon fires Rickey as manager and appoints Hornsby to take his place. Rickey remains the team's vice president and farm system director.

Sept. 27—Hornsby has five hits in a doubleheader against Boston, including his 38th and 39th homers, to raise his average to .403, the sixth consecutive year he leads the league in hitting. Hornsby sits out the final three games with a sore toe but the Cardinals go 64-51 with him as manager and finish the season 77-76, good for fourth in the league. Hornsby wins his second Triple Crown (.403, 39 HR, 143 RBIs) and becomes the first Cardinal to win a National League Most Valuable Player Award.

1926

June 22—The Cardinals acquire ▶ **Grover Cleveland Alexander** off waivers from the Cubs.

Aug. 31—The Cardinals move into first place with a doubleheader sweep of the Pirates at Sportsman's Park.

Sept. 8—Hornsby goes into an obscenity-laced tirade against Breadon after the owner tells him he wants the team to play in a pair of exhibition games in New Haven, Conn. It's the foundation for Hornsby's eventual exit from the Cardinals.

Sept. 24—The Cardinals clinch their first N.L. pennant with a 6-4 win over the Giants in New York. A few days later, they finish the season at 89-65.

Oct. 10—The Cardinals win their first World Series with a 3-2 victory over the Yankees in Game 7 in New York. Alexander becomes a hero when he comes out of the bullpen and strikes out Tony Lazzeri with the bases loaded and two outs in the seventh inning. The game ends with Babe Ruth being thrown out while attempting to steal second base.

▶ **Dec. 5**—Catcher **Bob O'Farrell** is named N.L. MVP. Later in the month, he is named manager, succeeding Hornsby.

Dec. 20—The Cardinals trade Hornsby to the Giants for second baseman Frankie Frisch and pitcher Jimmy Ring.

1927

May 14—The Cardinals lose, 12-4, at Philadelphia's Baker Bowl, but the game is remembered for another reason. In the seventh inning, a section of the right-field stands—full of fans—collapses, injuring about 50 people and causing another to suffer a fatal heart attack.

June 18—After aviation hero Charles Lindbergh helps to raise the team's N.L. pennant in pregame ceremonies at Sportsman's Park, the Cardinals lower the boom on the visiting Giants, 6-4.

Sept. 29—The Cardinals' hopes of repeating as World Series champions officially end with a 3-2 loss at Cincinnati. With a record of 92-61, they finish 1½ games behind Pittsburgh. Frisch strikes out just 10 times in 153 games, leads the N.L. in stolen bases (48) and finishes second in MVP voting in his first St. Louis season.

Nov. 7—Bill McKechnie, manager of the Cardinals' Rochester farm club, replaces O'Farrell as manager.

1928

Apr. 12—Alexander beats Pittsburgh, 9-0, at Sportsman's Park. It is the 90th and final shutout of his career—a N.L. record.

Sept. 20—In the first game of a doubleheader in New York, George Harper has the first three-homer game in Cardinals history.

Sept. 29—The Cardinals clinch their second N.L. pennant in three seasons with a 3-1 victory at Boston. They finish the season with a record of 95-59 and set a club record for home attendance (761,574).

Oct. 9—Babe Ruth swats three homers in a 7-3 Yankees victory at Sportsman's Park as New York completes a World Series sweep of the Cardinals.

Nov. 21—Billy Southworth replaces McKechnie as manager.

Dec. 2—Bottomley, who leads the N.L. in triples and RBIs and finishes tied in home runs, is voted N.L. MVP.

1929

July 6—The Cardinals end an 11-game losing streak with a 28-6 victory in the second game of a doubleheader at Philadelphia, setting a modern-day N.L. record for runs and hits (28). The beneficiary of the onslaught, starting pitcher Fred Frankhouse, has four hits, as does Bottomley. Center fielder/leadoff man Taylor Douthit leads the way with five.

July 9—Chick Hafey ties an N.L. record with his 10th consecutive hit over two games in a 7-4 victory over the Phillies.

July 24—Oh, never mind: McKechnie, who had been replaced as manager by Southworth the previous November, replaces the deposed Southworth on the St. Louis bench.

Aug. 10—Alexander beats the team he began his career with—the Phillies—for his 373rd and final big-league win. He pitches four scoreless innings in relief before the Cardinals push across two runs in the 11th inning for an 11-9 victory. Alexander's career win total equals Mathewson's N.L. record.

Sept. 29—The Cardinals beat the Pirates 10-2 at Sportsman's Park to finish a disappointing season at 78-74, 20 games out of first.

1930

Sept. 16—The Cardinals hand Brooklyn its first loss in 11 games—1-0 at Ebbets Field—to move into a first-place tie with the Dodgers. Pitching with a bandaged finger sticking out of his glove, Cardinals lefthander Bill Hallahan retires the first 20 batters he faces and holds the Dodgers to five hits in a complete-game victory.

Sept. 26—The Cardinals clinch the N.L. pennant with a 10-5 victory over Pittsburgh at Sportsman's Park.

Sept. 28—Dizzy Dean makes his major league debut on the final day of the season and throws a three-hitter to beat Pittsburgh, 3-1. Dean also singles and steals home in the third inning. While Dean has an impressive debut game,

outfielder George Watkins has an impressive debut season—his .373 batting average is the highest ever by a major league rookie. Watkins, however, does not lead the league; Giants first baseman Bill Terry hits a robust .401. Eleven Cardinals, including Watkins, hit .300 or better. The Cardinals finish the season with a record of 92-62 and win their third N.L. pennant.

Oct. 8—The Cardinals lose the World Series in six games to the Philadelphia Athletics. An offense that produces a team-record 1,004 runs during the regular season scores just one run in the final 22 innings against the A's.

SOUTHWORTH

1931

Aug. 5—**Bottomley** has a day to remember against the Pirates. After getting four hits in the first game of a double-header, he goes 6-for-6 in the nightcap.

Sept. 16—The Cardinals clinch the N.L. pennant—their fourth in six seasons—with a 6-3 victory over the Phillies at Sportsman's Park.

Sept. 27—Hafey goes 1 for 8 on the final day of the season to win the closest batting race ever. Hafey's .3489 average edges out New York's Terry (.3486) and teammate Bottomley (.3482). The Cards finish with a record of 101-53, their first 100-win year.

Oct. 10—The Cardinals, now managed by Gabby Street, prevent the Athletics from winning three consecutive World Series by beating Philadelphia, 4-2, in Game 7. Hallahan rescues a faltering Grimes, heretofore a World Series hero, after the A's put two runners on base with two outs in the ninth. Pepper Martin is the Series star for St. Louis, hitting .500 with five runs, five RBIs and five stolen bases.

Oct. 20—**Frisch** (.311, 28 steals, 82 RBIs) is selected N.L. MVP.

1932

Apr. 11—Hafey, fresh off his 1931 N.L. batting title, is traded to the Reds.

May 11—Hallahan lives up to his "Wild Bill" nickname by throwing a record-tying three wild pitches in one inning in a loss to Brooklyn.

Aug. 14—The Cardinals sweep a doubleheader from the Cubs at Sportsman's Park behind superb pitching by rookies Tex Carleton and Dizzy Dean.

Sept. 2—Joe Medwick makes his major league debut.

Sept. 25—The Cardinals fall to 72-82—their first losing season since 1924—and finish 18 games behind pennant-winning Chicago.

Oct. 24—Hornsby is signed by the Cardinals after being released by the Cubs. He plays in 46 games for St. Louis in 1933 and hits .325.

Dec. 17—Bottomley joins former teammate Hafey in Cincinnati as he is traded to the Reds. Like Hornsby, Bottomley will finish his playing career as a member of the A.L.'s St. Louis Browns in 1937.

1933

May 7—The Cardinals make a multi-player deal with the Reds and acquire light-hitting, fiery shortstop Leo Durocher.

July 2—The Cardinals fail to score a run while losing both ends of a doubleheader to the first-place Giants. Both games end 1-0 as Carl Hubbell (18) and Roy Parmelee (nine) do not allow a run in a combined 27 innings.

July 6—The Cardinals are well-represented at baseball's first All-Star Game as Frisch, Hallahan, Martin and catcher Jim Wilson all play in the game at Chicago's Comiskey Park. Frisch hits a homer for the N.L., the first of 13 that will be hit by Cardinal players in All-Star Games.

July 24—Street quits as manager and Frisch takes over. The team responds by winning 16 of its next 17 games.

July 30—Dean sets a modern major league record with 17 strikeouts in an 8-2 victory over the Cubs.

Oct. 1—The Cardinals go 82-71 and finish in fifth place despite a solid season by Dean, who wins 20 games for the first time.

1934

Sept. 16—The Cardinals sweep a doubleheader from the first-place Giants before a record crowd of 62,573 at the Polo Grounds, courtesy of the **Dean brothers**. Dizzy wins the first game, 5-3, and Paul takes the second 3-1.

Sept. 21—Dizzy throws a three-hit shutout against the Dodgers in the first game of a doubleheader in Brooklyn but is upstaged by Paul, who throws a 3-0 no-hitter in the second game.

Sept. 30—The Cardinals clinch the N.L. pennant on the final day of the season. Dizzy shuts out the Reds, 9-0, at Sportsman's Park for his 30th victory of the season. The Cardinals finish 95-58, two games ahead of New York.

Oct. 9—The Cardinals win the World Series by clobbering the Tigers, 11-0, in Game 7. Fans toss garbage at left fielder Medwick, who slid high into third baseman Marv Owen in the top of the sixth, when he takes the field for the bottom of the inning. In an effort to restore order, commissioner Kenesaw Mountain Landis orders Medwick removed from the game. The Dean brothers account for all four Series wins for St. Louis.

Nov. 3—Dizzy is named N.L. MVP after leading the league in wins, strikeouts (195) and shutouts (seven).

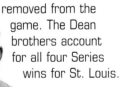

PAUL AND DIZZY DEAN

1935

July 18—The Cardinals pound out 18 hits and Paul Dean pitches a complete game in a 13-3 romp over the Boston Braves at Sportsman's Park. It is the Cardinals' 18th straight win at home and 14th straight win overall. Burgess Whitehead and Rip Collins pace the team with four hits each.

July 31—At Cincinnati, a female fan, Kitty Burke, runs on the field and grabs a bat from Reds outfielder Babe Herman as he is about to face Paul Dean. Burke hits a slow underhand toss back to the mound, and Dean throws her out at first. Frisch insists the out should count, but the umpires overrule him.

Sept. 5—Rookie Terry Moore becomes the first player in Cardinals history to go 6-for-6 in a home game.

Sept. 27—The Cubs, battling St. Louis for the pennant, sweep a doubleheader from St. Louis at Sportsman's Park to stretch their winning streak to 21 games. The win in the opener clinches the flag for Chicago. The Cardinals end the season two days later at 96-58.

1936

Apr. 14—On opening day in St. Louis, Eddie Morgan makes baseball history, becoming the first player to hit a pinch-hit home run in his first major league at-bat. It is the only homer Morgan hits in 39 big-league games.

Apr. 16—**Johnny Mize** makes his major league debut.

July 7—The N.L. wins its first All-Star Game, 4-3, at Braves Field in Boston as two Cardinals make major contributions. **Medwick** drives in what turns out to be the winning run in the fifth inning and Dizzy Dean, the N.L.'s starting pitcher, allows no hits in three innings to earn the victory.

July 21—Medwick ties a N.L. record when he singles in his first three at-bats against the Giants to stretch his consecutive-hit streak to 10.

Sept. 25—Medwick hits his 64th double of the season—a club record that still stands.

Sept. 27—On the season's final day, Walter Alston, who will later manage the Dodgers for 23 seasons, replaces Mize (ejected from the game) at first base and strikes out in his only major league at-bat. Cards go 87-67 and tie for second place.

1937

June 5—The Cardinals sign 16-year old pitcher **Stan Musial** to a professional contract.

July 7—At the All-Star Game in Washington, Cleveland's Earl Averill hits a line drive that breaks Dizzy Dean's left big toe. Dean returns from the injury in September but the toe isn't fully healed. As a result, he alters his motion and injures his shoulder. Medwick sets an All-Star record with four hits.

Aug. 4—The Cardinals score five runs in the ninth to pull out a 7-6 win over Boston in St. Louis. The final two runs come home on a pinch single by Frisch, his final career hit. Medwick hits four doubles.

Oct. 3—The Cardinals, 81-73, finish fourth. Medwick wins the Triple Crown with a .374 average, 31 homers and a club-record 154 RBIs. A month later he is voted N.L. MVP.

1938

MUSIAL

Jan. 18—Grover Cleveland Alexander, a Cardinal from 1926-29, is elected to the Baseball Hall of Fame.

Apr. 16—The Cardinals trade Dizzy Dean to the Cubs for outfielder Tuck Stainback, pitchers Curt Davis and Clyde Shoun and $185,000. Dean, still just 27 years old, will win only 16 games the rest of his career.

Apr. 19—Enos Slaughter makes his major league debut.

Aug. 2—The Cardinals lose 6-2 to the Dodgers at Ebbets Field in the first game in which yellow-colored baseballs are used. The new balls are best described by Mize, who hits one of them for a homer, as looking like "stitched lemons."

Sept. 11—Frisch is fired as manager following a 6-4 win over the Pirates. The Cardinals, in sixth place at the time, appoint coach Mike Gonzalez to take over for the rest of the season.

Oct. 2—The Cardinals finish 71-80 and fall to sixth place, 17½ games behind first-place Chicago.

Nov. 6—Former outfielder Ray Blades, a favorite of Rickey's, is named manager of the Cardinals.

1939

Aug. 16—Moore hits a pair of inside-the-park homers against the Pirates at Forbes Field.

Aug. 20—The Cardinals sweep a doubleheader from the Reds at Crosley Field, pull within 3½ games of the Reds in the N.L. race. Martin has three hits in each game and Mize hits two homers in the nightcap.

Sept. 28—A 5-3 loss to the Reds eliminates the Cardinals from pennant contention.

Oct. 1—The Cardinals finish in second place—4½ games behind first-place Cincinnati—with a 92-61 record. Mize wins the batting title (.349) and leads the N.L. in slugging average (.626) and homers (28) as well. Slaughter, at age 23, hits .320 and leads the league with 52 doubles. Davis, one of the players acquired for Dizzy Dean the previous year, wins 22 games.

1940

May 7—The Cards hit seven homers, rout Brooklyn, 18-2.

June 4—The Cardinals lose to Brooklyn, 10-1, in their first night game in St. Louis. Medwick goes 5-for-5.

June 7—Breadon fires Blades and asks minor league manager Southworth, who had been Card manager briefly in 1929, to take back his old job.

June 12—The Cardinals trade Medwick and Davis to the Dodgers for four players and $125,000. When the clubs meet six days later at Ebbets Field, Cards pitcher Bob Bowman beans Medwick, who is knocked unconscious. The incident sets off a long feud between the two clubs.

Sept. 29—The Cards finish third at 84-69. Mize leads the N.L. with 137 RBIs and a club-record 43 homers.

1942

HALL OF FAME

1942

Rogers Hornsby

Jan. 4—**Rogers Hornsby**, a Cardinal from 1915-26 and in 1933, is elected to the Baseball Hall of Fame.

Sept. 27—The Cardinals clinch the N.L. pennant on the final day of the season with a doubleheader sweep of the Cubs and finish two games ahead of Brooklyn at 106-48.

Oct. 3—Lefthander Ernie White shuts out New York, 2-0, in Game 3 of the World Series at Yankee Stadium to give St. Louis a two games-to-one lead.

Oct. 5—Slaughter hits a solo homer and rookie third baseman Whitey Kurowski adds a two-run shot in the ninth inning as the Cardinals win, 4-2, to beat the heavily favored Yankees in five games. It is New York's first World Series loss since the Cardinals beat them in 1926.

Oct. 29—Rickey resigns as Cardinals vice president and farm system director. Three days later he signs a five-year contract to head up Brooklyn's baseball operations.

Nov.—Righthanded pitcher **Mort Cooper**, who leads the league in wins, shutouts and ERA, is named N.L. MVP.

1943

Feb. 24—Because so many of their minor leaguers have enlisted or been drafted, the Cardinals reduce their farm system from 21 teams to seven. The next day, the team places a want ad in The Sporting News looking for young players.

May 31—Cooper allows just one hit—a looping double down the right-field foul line—in a 7-0 win over Brooklyn. Cooper throws another one-hitter in his next start against Philadelphia on June 4.

Sept. 18—The Cardinals clinch their second N.L. consecutive pennant with a doubleheader sweep of the Cubs in St. Louis. A couple of weeks later, they end the season with a 105-49 record. Musial hits .357 to win his first batting title.

Oct. 11—The Yankees avenge their 1942 defeat by beating the Cardinals, 2-0, to close out the World Series in five games. The Cardinals score two or fewer runs in each of their four losses.

Nov.—Musial, who leads the league in hits, doubles and triples as well as batting average, is named N.L. MVP.

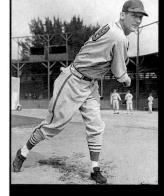

1941

Aug. 10—Slaughter breaks his collarbone in an outfield collision with Moore and misses the remainder of the year.

Aug. 30—**Lou Warneke** throws a 2-0 no-hitter at Cincinnati. Only three balls hit by the Reds make it to the outfield.

Sept. 17—In the second game of a doubleheader against the Braves at Sportsman's Park, Musial makes his major league debut. After popping out to third base in his first at-bat, he gets two hits in his next three at-bats, including a double. The Cards beat manager Casey Stengel's Braves, 3-2.

Sept. 23—Musial hits the first of 475 career homers in a 9-0 victory at Pittsburgh.

Sept. 29—On the final day of the season, Musial has five hits, steals a base and throws out two runners. The 97-56 Cardinals wind up the season in second place, 2½ games behind Brooklyn.

Dec. 11—The Cardinals trade Mize to the Giants for three nondescript players and $50,000.

1944

June 10—Cooper tosses a five-hit shutout as the Cardinals clobber Cincinnati, 18-0. The hometown Reds become so desperate that they literally send a hometown kid to the mound—lefthanded pitching prospect Joe Nuxhall, who at 15 years, 10 months and 11 days becomes the youngest player ever to appear in a major league game.

Sept. 21—The Cardinals clinch their third consecutive N.L. pennant with a 5-4 victory over Boston. Nine days later they finish the season with a 105-49 record, giving them 316 victories in the past three seasons.

Oct. 9—The Cardinals beat the Browns in an all-St. Louis World Series with a 3-1 victory in Game 6. The Cardinals hold their city rivals to just two runs in the final three games.

Dec. 21—Shortstop and defensive whiz **Marty Marion** is voted N.L. MVP. He also is named Major League Player of the Year by The Sporting News, the first Cardinal so honored.

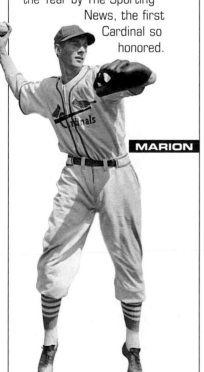

MARION

1945

Jan. 22—**Musial** enlists in the service and misses the entire 1945 season. The Cardinals recall infielder Albert "Red" Schoendienst from their Rochester farm team.

Apr. 17—Schoendienst makes his major league debut. He sees heavy outfield duty in '45.

May 23—The Cardinals trade Cooper, a three-time 20-game winner, to the Braves.

July 4—Outfielder Augie Bergamo bangs out 10 hits as the Cardinals sweep a doubleheader at the Polo Grounds, 8-4 and 9-2.

Sept. 30—The Cardinals go 95-59 and finish three games behind the N.L. champion Cubs. With Musial gone, Kurowski leads the team in batting (.323), homers (21) and RBIs (102). After the season, Southworth receives a lucrative offer to manage the Boston Braves and is replaced by **Eddie Dyer**.

1946

Aug. 12—Musial goes 4-for-4 in a 5-0 victory at Chicago to give him 12 hits in 13 at-bats over three games.

Sept. 29—The Cardinals miss a chance to win the pennant on the season's final day when they lose, 8-3, to the Cubs at Sportsman's Park and finish tied for first with Brooklyn at 96-58. A best-of-three playoff is scheduled.

Oct. 3—The Cardinals, after winning the first game, 4-2, build an early 8-1 and cruise to an 8-4 victory and two-game playoff sweep of the Dodgers.

Oct. 15—In one of the most famous plays in World Series history, **Slaughter** makes a "Mad Dash" from first base to score on Harry Walker's double in the eighth inning, giving the Cardinals a 4-3 victory over the Red Sox in Game 7.

Nov. 22—Musial wins his second N.L. MVP award. He also is named Major League Player of the Year by The Sporting News.

1947

HALL OF FAME

1947

Frankie Frisch

Jan. 21—**Frankie Frisch**, a Cardinal from 1927-37, is elected to thel Hall of Fame.

June 9—Schoendienst is 0-for-12 in a doubleheader against the Phillies.

July 30—Down 10-0 after four innings, the Cardinals score six runs with two outs in the bottom of the ninth against visiting Brooklyn to tie the game at 10-10 and send it into extra innings. The Dodgers, however, win the game when Pee Wee Reese singles home Gene Hermanski in the top of the 10th inning.

Sept. 27—The 89-65 Cardinals finish second—five games back of Brooklyn.

Nov. 25—Breadon sells the Cardinals to a couple of local businessmen—attorney Fred Saigh and Postmaster **General Bob Hannegan.**

EDDIE DYER, LEFT, WITH HANNEGAN

239

1948

June 6—In a doubleheader sweep of the Phillies, **Schoendienst** ties an N.L. record with five doubles. Combined with his three doubles the previous day, he sets a major league record with eight doubles over a three-game span. Four Cardinals—Erv Dusak, Schoendienst, Slaughter and Nippy Jones—hit homers in the sixth inning of the first game.

July 13—St. Louis hosts the All-Star Game and Musial thrills local fans with a first-inning homer.

Aug. 29—Jackie Robinson hits for the cycle as the Dodgers beat the Cardinals 12-7 at Sportsman's Park.

Sept. 22—Musial ties a record held by Ty Cobb with his fourth five-hit game of the season when he homers, doubles and singles three times in an 8-2 victory over the Braves.

Oct. 3—The Cardinals end the season in second place at 85-69. Musial leads the N.L. in every hitting department except home runs.

Nov.—Musial wins his third and final N.L. MVP Award.

1949

May 10—Breadon, owner of the Cardinals from 1920 to 1947, dies of cancer at the age of 72.

July 24—The one and only: Musial hits for the cycle for the only time in his career.

Sept. 29—The Cardinals fall out of first place following a 7-2 loss at Pittsburgh.

Oct. 2—The Cardinals beat the Cubs, 13-5, at Wrigley Field on the final day of the season but lose the N.L. pennant by one game when Brooklyn beats the Phillies, 9-7, in 10 innings. St. Louis loses six of its last nine games to finish 96-58. Nevertheless, the 1940s turn out to be the winningest decade in franchise history. From 1940 through 1949, the Cardinals win 960 games and lose 580 (.623 winning percentage), with four pennants and three World Series championships.

1950

April 18—The Cardinals defeat the Pirates, 4-1, in the first opening-day night game in St. Louis.

May 18—Third baseman Tommy Glaviano makes four errors (three in the ninth inning) to help turn an 8-5 Cardinals lead into a 9-8 Dodgers win at Ebbets Field.

July 11—Schoendienst, an 11th-inning defensive replacement, gives the N.L. a 4-3 victory in the All-Star Game with a 14th-inning homer at Comiskey Park.

July 27—Musial has a 30-game hitting streak—the longest in the majors in the 1950s—end when he is the only Cardinal to go hitless in a 13-3 romp over Brooklyn.

Oct. 1—The Cardinals end the season in fifth place at 78-75. Musial hits .356 and wins the batting title.

Oct. 16—Dyer resigns as manager and is replaced by Marion.

1951

Sept. 13—The Cardinals become the first team in the 20th century to play two different teams on the same day in the same ballpark as they host the Giants and Braves at Sportsman's Park. Neither game, ironically, was on the schedule at the beginning of the season. After beating the Giants 6-4 in the opener, a makeup game from the night before, the Cardinals are beaten by the Braves, 2-0, in a makeup game from earlier in the season. Twenty-game winner Sal Maglie takes the loss in the opener for New York while 20-game winner Warren Spahn wins the nightcap for Boston.

Sept. 30—The Cardinals split a doubleheader at Chicago and finish in third place at 81-73. Musial hits .355 to win his second straight batting title. Marion is fired as manager and replaced by ▶ **Eddie Stanky.**

Nov.—Musial is named Major League Player of the Year by The Sporting News.

1952

June 15—The Cardinals rally from an 11-0 deficit to beat the Giants 14-12 in the first game of a doubleheader at the Polo Grounds. It is the largest comeback ever by an National League team. Slaughter (five RBIs) and Solly Hemus (two home runs) pace the St. Louis attack.

Sept. 28—In the season finale, Musial makes his only big-league pitching appearance. The only batter he faces, the Cubs' Frankie Baumholtz, turns around and bats righthanded and reaches on an error by third baseman Hemus. Stan is then relieved by the man he replaced, starting pitcher Harvey Haddix (who had moved to the outfield). Musial goes 1-for-3 in the game and wins his third straight batting title, his .336 average topping Baumholtz by 11 points. The 88-66 Cards finish in third place.

1953

HALL OF FAME

1953

Dizzy Dean

Jan. 21—Dizzy Dean, a Cardinal in 1930 and from 1932-37, is elected to the Baseball Hall of Fame.

Jan. 28—Saigh is sentenced to 15 months in prison and fined $15,000 on charges of income tax evasion. He puts the club up for sale.

BUSCH AND COMPANY

Feb. 20—Anheuser-Busch buys the Cardinals from Saigh for $3.75 million.

April 9—Browns owner Bill Veeck sells Sportsman's Park to Anheuser-Busch Inc. for $800,000. **August A. Busch Jr.** wants to rename the stadium Budweiser Park, settles for Busch Stadium.

Sept. 25— Cardinals rookie Harvey Haddix wins No. 20.

Sept. 27—The Cards finish in a tie for third at 83-71. Ray Jablonski hits 21 home runs, a club rookie record.

1954

Apr. 11—Slaughter is dealt to the Yankees for outfielders Bill Virdon and Emil Tellinger and pitcher Mel Wright.

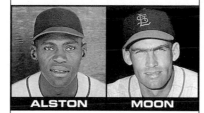

ALSTON **MOON**

Apr. 13—It's a day of firsts at Busch Stadium: First baseman **Tom Alston** (above left) becomes the first black player in Cardinals history and outfielder **Wally Moon** homers in his first big-league at-bat.

Apr. 23—It's another first: In his seventh game, Milwaukee rookie Hank Aaron hits his first career homer—a seventh-inning shot off Cards righthander Vic Raschi.

May 2—Musial hits five home runs in a doubleheader against the Giants in St. Louis, connecting three times in the first game and twice in the second. Alston is 4-for-4 in the opener but few notice.

Sept. 26—The Cardinals finish 72-82 and drop to sixth place. Moon is named N.L. Rookie of the Year.

1955

May 27—Stanky wreaks havoc on the visiting clubhouse at Crosley Field after a loss to the Reds and is fired the next day by Busch. Rochester manager Harry Walker is hired as Stanky's replacement.

June 1—It's Rookie Day at Pittsburgh's Forbes Field as Ken Boyer and Bill Virdon get three hits apiece and lefthander Luis Arroyo pitches a six-hit, 6-2 victory over the Pirates. It is Arroyo's sixth win without a loss. Pittsburgh rookie Roberto Clemente goes 1-for-3 and drives in a run.

July 12—Musial wins the All-Star Game for the N.L. in dramatic fashion, 6-5, with a homer in the bottom of the 12th at Milwaukee's County Stadium.

Sept. 25—The Cardinals finish in seventh at 68-86—their lowest win total since 1924.

Oct. 6—The Cardinals hire Frank Lane as general manager. Six days later, Lane fires Walker and replaces him with Fred Hutchinson.

1956

G.M. Lane takes the birds-on-the-bat logo off the front of the Cardinals' uniforms. Fans are incensed. Familiar logo returns in 1957. Pictured at right is Don Blasingame, **who in the 1958 season replaces Schoendienst as the Cards' second baseman.**

June 14—One month after trading Virdon, the reigning N.L. Rookie of the Year, to Pittsburgh in a questionable deal, Lane lives up to his "Trader Lane" nickname by shipping four players, including Schoendienst, to the Giants for four players. Shortstop Alvin Dark and outfielder Whitey Lockman are among those who come to St. Louis.

July 9—The Sporting News selects Musial as its Player of the Decade for the 10-year period of 1946-55.

Sept. 30—One day after knocking the Milwaukee Braves out of first place, the Cardinals finish the season in fourth place at 76-78, 17 games behind the Dodgers.

Nov. 27—Outfielder **Charlie Peete**, winner of the 1956 American Association batting title, dies in a plane crash in Venezuela. The Cardinals prospect is killed 34 years to the day after Austin McHenry's death. Both were 27 years old.

1957

June 21—In his first career start, **Von McDaniel**, an 18-year-old righthander right out of high school, holds the Dodgers to two hits in a 2-0 win at Busch Stadium.

July 28—McDaniel narrowly misses a perfect game in the first game of a doubleheader against the Pirates at Busch Stadium. The only hitter to reach base against the Oklahoman is Pittsburgh's Gene Baker, who hits a bloop double down the left-field line in the second inning that left fielder Del Ennis can't track down.

Sept. 23—The Braves beat the Cardinals, 4-2, on a two-run homer by Aaron in the 11th inning to win the N.L. pennant. The Cardinals end the season a week later in second place at 87-67. Musial hits .351 to win his seventh and final batting title.

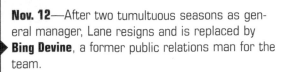

Nov. 12—After two tumultuous seasons as general manager, Lane resigns and is replaced by ▶ **Bing Devine**, a former public relations man for the team.

1958

Jan. 29—Musial signs a $100,000 contract, is highest-paid player in N.L. history.

May 13—At Wrigley Field, Musial, in a pinch-hitting role, doubles off Moe Drabowsky for career hit No. 3,000. Hutchinson had given Musial the day off in the hope he could get the milestone hit during a homestand that was to begin the next night.

Sept. 1—Lefthander **Vinegar Bend Mizell** walks nine batters in a 1-0 victory over the Reds. It's the most bases on balls ever issued by an N.L. pitcher in a shutout win.

Sept. 29—The Cardinals conclude the season in a tie for fifth place at 72-82. Hutchinson is dismissed.

1959

Apr. 16—New manager Solly Hemus uses a record 25 players in a 7-6 loss to the Dodgers in Los Angeles. One of them is 23-year-old righthander Bob Gibson, who allows three hits in just one-third of an inning. A day earlier Gibson gave up two homers in relief in his major league debut.

June 21—Musial hits the 652nd double of his career in a game against the Pirates to break Honus Wagner's N.L. record.

July 30—Gibson gets his first major league victory—a 1-0 shutout at Cincinnati.

Sept. 27—The Cardinals sweep a doubleheader from the Giants at Busch Stadium to end the season in seventh place at 71-83. One of the few highlights is outfielder

Joe Cunningham, who makes the N.L. All-Star team and hits .345 to finish second in the batting race.

1960

Jan. 21—Musial asks for and receives a $20,000 pay cut after what he feels was a subpar 1959 season.

Apr. 12—The Cardinals lose, 3-1, to the Giants in the inaugural game at San Francisco's Candlestick Park.

May 15—In the second game of a doubleheader at Wrigley Field, Chicago's Don Cardwell throws a 4-0 no-hitter against the Cardinals.

May 28—The Cardinals trade Mizell to the Pirates in a four-player deal that brings second baseman Julian Javier to St. Louis.

Oct. 2—The Cardinals jump to third place with an 86-68 record but finish nine games back of pennant-winning Pittsburgh.

1961

July 6—Hemus is fired as manager and replaced by coach **Johnny Keane**, a 17-year member of the St. Louis organization. The first thing Keane does is put Gibson in the starting rotation.

July 17-18—**Bill White** goes 14-for-18 in back-to-back doubleheaders against the Cubs. On the first day he is 8-for-10; in the second 6-for-8. White's 14 hits over two days tie a major league record held by Ty Cobb, who, ironically, dies on the first day of White's hitting

onslaught. The Cardinals win all four games.

Aug. 3—The Cardinals suffer their worst shutout defeat ever—a 19-0 shellacking at Pittsburgh.

Oct. 1—At 80-74, the Cardinals finish the season in fifth place, 13 games behind league champ Cincinnati.

1962

Apr. 11—The Cardinals beat New York, 11-4, at Busch Stadium in the Mets' debut game in the National League and hand future Cardinal Roger Craig the first of his league-high 24 defeats.

May 19—Musial gets career hit No. 3,431 to surpass Wagner for the top spot on the N.L.'s all-time hit list.

July 25—Musial drives in the 1,861st run of his career, breaking Mel Ott's N.L. record for RBIs.

Sept. 23—Maury Wills of the Dodgers ties and then breaks Cobb's long-standing record for most stolen bases in a season, getting his 96th and 97th in St. Louis.

Sept. 30—The Cardinals beat the Dodgers, 1-0, on a Gene Oliver home run to sweep a three-game series in Los Angeles. Oliver's shot forces a one-game playoff between the Dodgers and the Giants for the N.L. pennant. St. Louis finishes sixth in the new 10-team league at 84-78.

Nov. 19—Cards acquire shortstop Dick Groat, the 1960 N.L. MVP, from the Pirates.

Musial, known for his unusual but highly effective batting stance, celebrated with teammates (below) after he collected hit No. 3,431 and surpassed Honus Wagner as the all-time N.L. leader.

1963

Aug. 12—It's the end of an era: Musial announces his retirement, effective at the end of the season.

Sept. 18—The Dodgers beat the Cardinals, 6-5, in 13 innings at Busch Stadium to complete a three-game sweep and knock St. Louis out of the pennant race.

Sept. 25—The Cardinals announce Musial's No. 6 will be retired, the first Cardinal so honored. It also is announced that Musial will become a team vice president after the season.

Sept. 29—On Stan Musial Day at Busch Stadium, the future Hall of Famer gets two hits to bring his career total to 3,630, second only to Cobb. One of them is a single that eludes Reds second baseman Pete Rose, who later will accumulate a few hits of his own. At 93-69, Cards finish in second place.

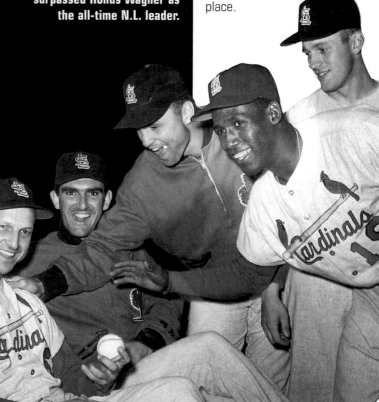

1964

June 15—With his team in eighth place and going nowhere, Devine makes his boldest trade, sending pitchers **Ernie Broglio** and Bobby Shantz and outfielder Doug Clemens to the Cubs for outfielder Lou Brock and two pitchers.

Aug. 16—**Curt Flood** gets hits in eight consecutive at-bats in a doubleheader vs. Los Angeles.

Aug. 17—Busch fires Devine and appoints Bob Howsam general manager.

Oct. 4—On the final day of the season, the Cardinals beat the Mets, 11-5, to win their first N.L. pennant since 1946. Their 93-69 record places them one game ahead of the Phillies and the Reds. Boyer, the eventual N.L. MVP, leads the league with 119 RBIs. Brock hits .348 with 33 stolen bases after joining St. Louis.

Oct. 11—With the Cardinals down 2-1 in the World Series and 3-0 in the sixth inning of Game 4, Boyer hits a grand slam to give St. Louis a 4-3 victory over the Yankees at Yankee Stadium.

Oct. 12—Tim McCarver hits a three-run homer in the 10th inning to give the Cardinals a 5-2 win in Game 5.

Oct. 15—The Cardinals win their first World Series in 18 years with a 7-5 win in Game 7.

Oct. 16—In a bizarre series of events that begin this day, Keane, still upset with the firing of Devine and hearing rumors that Busch has been courting Leo Durocher to replace him in the Cardinal dugout, announces his resignation as manager. Keane then becomes manager of the team he just beat—the Yankees—following the dismissal of Yogi Berra in New York. Schoendienst is later named Keane's successor in St. Louis.

Cardinals fans rejoice after the team wins its first N.L. pennant since 1946.

1965

June 8—The Cardinals make righthanded pitcher Joe DiFabio their first-ever amateur draft pick. DiFabio never pitches in the majors.

Sept. 29—Gibson hits his fifth homer of the season—a grand slam off San Francisco's Gaylord Perry—in an 8-6 Cardinals win.

Oct. 3—The Cardinals win their season finale at Houston but finish in seventh place with a record of 80-81.

Oct. 20—The Cardinals trade Boyer, a World Series hero 12 months earlier, to the Mets for lefthander Al Jackson and infielder Charley Smith.

Oct. 27—The Cardinals trade White, Groat and catcher Bob Uecker to the Phillies for outfielder Alex Johnson, catcher Pat Corrales and righthander Art Mahaffey.

Dec. 8—Branch Rickey dies in Columbia, Mo., at age 83.

1966

May 8—The Cardinals play their final game at old Busch Stadium (formerly Sportsman's Park) and lose to the Giants, 10-5. They trade pitcher Ray Sadecki to the Giants for first baseman Orlando Cepeda.

May 12—The Cardinals open new Busch Memorial Stadium with a come-from-behind 4-3 victory over Atlanta in 12 innings. The crowd of 46,048 is a bit below capacity on a chilly night but nonetheless is the largest ever to see a sporting event in St. Louis.

Home plate is moved from old Busch Stadium to the new one.

July 12—The National League beats the American League, 2-1 in 10 innings, in the first All-Star Game held in St. Louis in nine years.

Sept. 28—Larry Jaster shuts out the Dodgers for the fifth time in five starts. In 45 innings against the St. Louis lefthander, the Dodgers get 24 hits, all singles. Jaster goes 6-5 with a 4.64 ERA against the rest of the league.

Oct. 3—The Cardinals finish the season in sixth place at 83-79.

Dec. 8—The Cardinals trade Smith to the Yankees for outfielder **Roger Maris**.

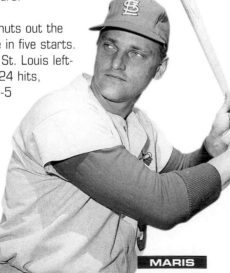

MARIS

GIBSON

1967

Jan. 23—Howsam resigns as general manager and is replaced by Musial.

July 15—A vicious line drive off the bat of Pittsburgh's Roberto Clemente breaks **Gibson**'s right leg in a 6-4 loss to Pittsburgh.

Sept. 18—Gibson, in his third start since the injury, clinches the pennant for the Cards by beating the Phillies, 5-1, at Philadelphia.

Oct. 1—The Cardinals beat Atlanta, 5-2, to finish with their first 100-win season in 23 years (101-60). Cepeda will later be voted the first unanimous N.L. MVP.

Oct. 12—The Cardinals beat the Red Sox, 7-2, in Game 7 of the World Series at Fenway Park as Gibson homers and strikes out 10. It is his third complete game of the Series.

Dec. 5—**Musial** (left) resigns as general manager and is replaced by **Devine**. Musial remains with the team as a senior vice president and consultant.

1968

Jan. 23—**Joe Medwick**, a Cardinal from 1932-40 and 1947-48, is elected to the Baseball Hall of Fame.

HALL OF FAME
1968
Joe Medwick

Aug. 19—Gibson wins his 15th game in a row. The streak includes five consecutive shutouts.

Sept. 18—Ray Washburn throws a no-hitter against the Giants in San Francisco, one day after the Giants' Gaylord Perry no-hits the Cards.

Sept. 27—In his final start of the season, Gibson hurls 13th shutout and lowers his ERA to a record 1.12. Two days later, the Cards finish at 97-65.

Oct. 2—In Game 1 of the World Series, Gibson strikes out 17 Tigers, a Series record.

Oct. 11—The Tigers rally from a three-games-to-one deficit to win the World Series.

Oct. 28—Gibson is unanimously voted the N.L. Cy Young Award and later is named N.L. MVP.

1969

HALL OF FAME
1969
Stan Musial

Jan. 21—**Stan Musial**, a Cardinal from 1941-63, is elected to the Baseball Hall of Fame.

Mar. 17—The Cardinals trade former MVP Cepeda to the Braves for catcher/first baseman **Joe Torre**, a future MVP.

Apr. 14—Light-hitting shortstop Dal Maxvill stuns the baseball world by hitting the first home run in the first major league game ever played in Canada. But the Cardinals still lose, 8-7, to the Expos at Montreal's Jarry Park.

Sept. 15—Steve Carlton sets a major league record with 19 strikeouts in a game against the Mets at Busch Stadium but loses, 4-3, as Ron Swoboda hits a pair of two-run homers.

Oct. 2—In baseball's first season of divisional play, the Cardinals finish fourth in the six-team N.L. East at 87-75.

Oct. 7—The Cardinals trade Flood, McCarver, pitcher Joe Hoerner and outfielder Byron Browne to the Phillies for first baseman Dick Allen, pitcher Jerry Johnson and infielder Cookie Rojas. Flood, after 12 seasons with the Cardinals, refuses to be a part of the deal and decides to take the matter to court.

1970

HALL OF FAME
1970
Jesse Haines

Feb 1.—**Jesse Haines**, a Cardinal from 1920-37, is elected to the Hall of Fame by the Veterans Committee.

Jan. 16—Flood files a suit challenging major league baseball's reserve clause.

Mar. 10—Synthetic turf is installed at Busch Stadium.

Apr. 26—Gibson strikes out 15 batters, including six in succession, in a 4-1 victory over the Reds.

May 21—Carlton strikes out 16 but gets no decision in a 4-3 St. Louis loss at Philadelphia. Two days later, Gibson strikes out 16 Phillies and the Cardinals win 3-1 on a pair of homers by Allen.

Oct. 1—Cards lose to the Pirates, finish fourth (76-86). A month later, Gibson (23-7, 3.12 ERA) wins his second Cy Young Award.

1971

1971

Chick Hafey

Jan. 31—**Chick Hafey**, a Cardinal from 1924-31, is elected to the Baseball Hall of Fame by the Veterans Committee.

June 8—The Cardinals take first baseman **Keith Hernandez** in the 42nd round of the amateur draft.

Aug. 4—Gibson gets career victory No. 200 in a 7-2 win over the Giants in St. Louis.

Aug. 14—Gibson, who will finish his career with two one-hitters, eight two-hitters and 24 three-hitters, pitches his only no-hitter, an 11-0 rout of the Pirates. The Cardinals score five runs in the top of the first inning to give their ace an early lead. Gibson strikes out one of the most feared batsmen in the game, Willie Stargell, for the final out.

Sept. 30—The Cardinals finish second in the N.L. East with a record of 90-72. Torre hits .363 to win the batting title and leads the league with 137 RBIs. He is voted N.L. MVP on November 10 and is later named Major League Player of the Year by The Sporting News.

1972

Feb. 25—The Cardinals make perhaps their worst trade as they send Carlton—embroiled in a contract dispute with owner Gussie Busch—to the Phillies for righthander **Rick Wise**. Wise is gone from St. Louis within two years while Carlton wins four Cy Young Awards with Philadelphia.

Apr. 15—Another bad trade: The Cardinals deal lefthanded pitcher Jerry Reuss, a St. Louis native, to the Astros for righthander Scipio Spinks and lefthander Lance Clemons. Reuss will go on to win 220 games over 22 big-league seasons while Spinks and Clemons will combine for nine career wins.

Aug. 29—Giants pitcher Jim Barr retires the first 20 batters he faces in a 3-0 win over the Cardinals, stretching his string of consecutive batters retired to a major league record 41.

Oct. 4—The Cardinals beat the Pirates, 4-3, in Pittsburgh to finish in fourth place at 75-81. Gibson, in addition to winning 19 games, hits five home runs, just 11 fewer than team leader Ted Simmons.

1973

June 13—Wise is two outs away from a no-hitter before giving up a single to the Reds' Joe Morgan. The Cardinals win, 8-0, as Simmons goes 4-for-5 and Luis Melendez hits a grand slam.

Sept. 29—Gibson and the Cardinals beat Carlton and the Phillies, 7-1. The Cardinals end the season the following day at 81-81. Still, they finish only 1½ games behind the first-place Mets.

Oct. 26—Devine trades Wise and outfielder Bernie Carbo to the Red Sox for outfielder Reggie Smith and pitcher Ken Tatum.

1974

Jan. 28—**Jim Bottomley**, a Cardinal from 1922-32, is elected to the Baseball Hall of Fame by the Veterans Committee.

1974

Jim Bottomley

July 17—Gibson strikes out Cincinnati's Cesar Geronimo for his 3,000th career strikeout, the only pitcher other than Walter Johnson to reach the 3,000 mark. On the same day, former Cardinals great Dizzy Dean dies at age 63 in Reno, Nev.

Sept. 10—It's a bad day for Maury Wills and Max Carey at Busch Stadium as Brock steals his 104th and 105th bases of the season to first tie and then break Wills' single-season record. The two steals give Lou 740 in his career, breaking Carey's longstanding N.L. record.

Sept. 11—The Cardinals and Mets play on and on at Shea Stadium before rookie **Bake McBride** scores the winning run from first base on two Mets errors to give St. Louis a 4-3 win in 25 innings.

Oct. 2—The 86-75 Cardinals, trailing the Pirates by one game, are snowed out in their season finale with Montreal. A makeup game isn't necessary as the Pirates beat the Cubs in extra innings to win the N.L. East.

Nov. 27—McBride is voted N.L. Rookie of the Year. Brock, on the heels of his record-breaking 118-steal season, is later named Major League Player of the Year by The Sporting News.

1975

Sept. 1—Gibson, who has announced this will be his last season, is honored on Bob Gibson Day in front of a sellout crowd at Busch Stadium. He makes his final pitching appearance in relief two days later and ends his career with 251 victories, 3,117 strikeouts and a record 303 consecutive starts.

Sept. 28—The Cardinals end an 82-80 season with a 6-2 victory over division champion Pittsburgh to finish in a tie for third place.

1976

Apr. 19—McBride goes 5-for-8 at the plate in a 4-3, 17-inning loss to the Mets.

May 22—Smith hits three homers and drives in five runs in leading the Cardinals to a 7-6 win at Philadelphia.

Oct. 3—The Cardinals close out a miserable season by being shut out, 1-0, in both ends of a doubleheader against Pittsburgh. The Cardinals, who also were shut out, 8-0, the day before, end the season with a four-game losing streak and finish with a record of 72-90. It is St. Louis' first 90-loss season since 1916. Schoendienst subsequently is fired after 12 seasons as manager and replaced by minor league manager **Vern Rapp**.

1977

May 9—Lefthanded reliever Al Hrabosky walks the tightrope twice and survives both times as he defeats the defending World Series champion Reds, 6-5, in a 10-inning game at Busch Stadium. After the Reds load the bases with none out in the ninth inning, the "Mad Hungarian" strikes out George Foster, Johnny Bench and Bob Bailey in succession. Hrabosky escapes another jam in the 10th, then Ted Simmons ends the game with a homer in the bottom of the inning.

Aug. 29—Brock breaks Ty Cobb's modern major league stolen-base record by swiping No. 893 in a 4-3 loss at San Diego.

Sept. 30—Brock gets steal No. 900 in a 7-2 victory over the Mets in the first game of a doubleheader at Busch Stadium.

Oct. 2—At 83-79, the Cards finish third, 18 games behind division titlist Philadelphia. Shortstop Garry Templeton ends his first full season with 18 triples, the most in the majors since 1957.

Dec. 8—The Cardinals trade Hrabosky to Kansas City for righthander Mark Littell and catcher Buck Martinez.

1978

Apr. 16—Bob Forsch throws the first no-hitter in Busch Stadium history as he beats the Phillies, 5-0. It is the first no-hitter thrown in St. Louis in 54 years.

Apr. 25—Rapp is fired and Jack Krol acts as interim manager until Boyer, who is managing at Class AAA Springfield, is hired April 29.

May 26—The Cardinals acquire outfielder **George Hendrick** from the Padres for righthander Eric Rasmussen.

May 30—Silvio Martinez, acquired from the White Sox the previous offseason, pitches an 8-2 one-hitter against the Mets in his first start in a Cardinals uniform. The rookie also one-hits Pittsburgh July 8 and throws a pair of two-hitters but finishes just 9-8.

June 16—Tom Seaver, now with the Reds, throws the only no-hitter of his career, 4-0, against St. Louis in Cincinnati.

Oct. 1—The Cardinals go 62-82 under Boyer and finish the season in fifth place at 69-93.

1979

May 1—With the Cardinals trailing Houston, 6-3, in the bottom of the 11th at Busch, pinch hitter Roger Freed hits an electrifying, game-winning grand slam with two out.

Aug. 13—Brock joins the 3,000-hit club when he lashes a line drive off the hand of Cubs righthander Dennis Lamp in a 3-2 victory at Busch Stadium. Almost overlooked is the major league debut of Tommy Herr.

Sept. 23—Brock steals the 938th and final base of his career in a 7-4 victory against the Mets at Shea Stadium and moves past turn-of-the-century player Billy Hamilton for No. 1 on the all-time list.

Sept. 28—Templeton gets three hits batting righthanded in a 7-6 loss to the Mets to give the switch-hitter 100 hits from each side of the plate, a major league first.

Sept. 30—The Cardinals improve to 86-76, finish third.

Nov. 13—Hernandez, the N.L.'s leading hitter (.344), is named co-MVP with Pittsburgh's Willie Stargell, the first time the award is split.

1980

June 8—Boyer is fired by G.M. John Claiborne between games of a doubleheader in Montreal, with Krol taking over as interim manager. The next day **Whitey Herzog**, who had won three division titles in Kansas City, is hired as the new St. Louis manager.

Aug. 29—Herzog replaces the since-fired Claiborne as general manager, with Schoendienst becoming interim manager.

Oct. 5—The Cardinals finish a forgettable season in fourth place, at 74-88.

Dec. 8—Herzog, now in the role of general manager and field manager, completes an 11-player deal with the Padres, with closer Rollie Fingers being St. Louis' biggest catch. Fingers, however, is a Cardinal for only four days before Herzog sends him, Simmons and pitcher Pete Vuckovich to the Brewers for outfielder Sixto Lezcano, pitchers Lary Sorensen and Dave LaPoint and minor league outfielder David Green. The acquisition of All-Star closer Bruce Sutter from the Cubs on December 9 makes Fingers expendable, while Simmons will soon be replaced by free-agent signee Darrell Porter, a Herzog favorite from his days with the Royals.

1981

Jan. 15—**Bob Gibson**, a Cardinal from 1959-75, is elected to the Hall of Fame. Two months later, the Veterans Committee adds **Johnny Mize**, a Cardinal from 1936-41.

June 7—The Cards trade outfielder Tony Scott to Houston for pitcher Joaquin Andujar.

June 12—The Major League Baseball Players Association goes on strike. Sport is shut down for nearly two months.

Aug. 26—Templeton makes an obscene gesture toward the stands after being ejected from a game against the Giants. Herzog fines Templeton and suspends him indefinitely. Templeton makes a public apology, but his days with the team are numbered.

Oct. 4—A regular season that is split in half because of the strike ends. The Cards' overall record of 59-43 is the best in the N.L. East, but they fail to finish first in either half and miss the postseason.

Nov. 20—In a three-way deal involving the Phillies and Indians, the Cardinals acquire outfielder Lonnie Smith.

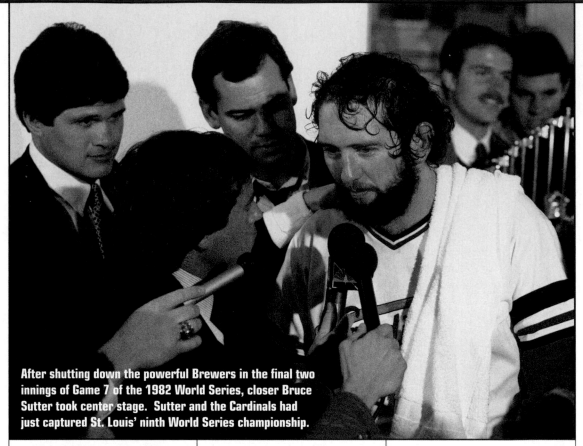

After shutting down the powerful Brewers in the final two innings of Game 7 of the 1982 World Series, closer Bruce Sutter took center stage. Sutter and the Cardinals had just captured St. Louis' ninth World Series championship.

1982

Feb. 11—The Cardinals trade Templeton to San Diego for shortstop Ozzie Smith.

Aug. 22—Third-string catcher Glenn Brummer—arguably the slowest player on the team—steals home with two out in the bottom of the 12th inning, giving the Cardinals a stunning 5-4 victory over the visiting San Francisco Giants.

Sept. 19—After sweeping a pair of doubleheaders the previous two days, the Cardinals beat the Mets for the fifth time in three days, 3-1, in New York. The latest win increases their lead over second-place Philadelphia to 4½ games.

Sept. 27—The Cardinals clinch their first N.L. East title with a 4-2 victory in Montreal. The game is highlighted by a three-run, inside-the-park homer by rookie outfielder Willie McGee. Six days later,

the Cardinals end the season with a 92-70 record.

Oct. 10—The Cardinals win, 6-2, in Atlanta to complete a three-game sweep of the Braves in the National League Championship Series.

Oct. 15—In Game 3 of the World Series at Milwaukee's County Stadium, McGee hits

two homers and takes two homers away from the Brewers with leaping catches at the wall in a 6-2 St. Louis victory.

Oct. 20—The Cardinals, down 3-1 in Game 7, rally for three runs in the sixth inning and go on to a 6-3 victory over Milwaukee for the franchise's ninth World Series championship.

1983

Apr. 6—Herzog steps down as general manager and Joe McDonald takes over. But the final decisions on all personnel matters still rest with Herzog.

June 15—In an unpopular trade, Herzog sends Hernandez to the Mets for pitchers Neil Allen and Rick Ownbey.

Sept. 23—Carlton, in yet another reminder for St. Louis fans of what might have been, beats the Cardinals, 6-2, at Busch Stadium for his 300th career win.

Sept. 26—Forsch becomes the only pitcher in Cardinals history to throw two no-hitters as he tames the Expos in a 3-0 win in St. Louis.

Oct. 2—The Cardinals fall to 79-83 and fourth place, but **Lonnie Smith** hits .321 to finish second in the N.L. batting race.

1984

May 12—Cincinnati righthander Mario Soto holds the Cardinals hitless until the ninth inning, when Hendrick—mired in a deep slump—spoils Soto's fun by swatting a two-out, two-strike homer. The Reds rally to win the game in the bottom of the ninth, 2-1.

June 23—In a nationally televised game at Wrigley Field, McGee and Cubs second baseman Ryne Sandberg put on an amazing hitting display in a game eventually won by Chicago, 12-11, in 11 innings. While McGee hits for the cycle and drives in six runs, Sandberg has five hits, seven RBIs and twice saves the Cubs from defeat by hitting game-tying homers off Sutter in the ninth and 10th innings.

Sept. 28—Sutter ties Dan Quisenberry's one-year-old major league record as he records his 45th save of the season in a 4-1 win over the Cubs.

Sept. 30—The Cardinals finish in third place at 84-78.

Dec. 7—Sutter signs a lucrative free-agent contract with Atlanta.

Dec. 12—The Cardinals trade Hendrick and minor league catcher Steve Barnard to the Pirates for lefthander **John Tudor** and catcher Brian Harper.

HALL OF FAME 1985
Lou Brock

HALL OF FAME 1985
Enos Slaughter

1985

Jan. 7—**Lou Brock**, a Cardinal from 1964-79, is elected to the Hall of Fame. Two months later, **Enos Slaughter**, a Cardinal from 1938-42 and 1946-53, is elected by the Veterans Committee.

Feb. 1—The Cardinals acquire first baseman Jack Clark from the Giants for four players.

Aug. 1—The Cards steal four bases on one pitch at Chicago as rookie Vince Coleman steals third and home and McGee second and third.

Sept. 11—Newly acquired Cesar Cedeno, subbing for the injured Clark, hits a 10th inning homer off Mets pitcher Jesse Orosco to give the Cardinals a crucial 1-0 win at Shea Stadium. The blast makes a winner of Tudor, who goes the distance for his third straight shutout, and moves St. Louis back into a tie with the Mets for first place. Cedeno winds up hitting .434 for the Cards in 28 games.

Oct. 5—Cards beat the Cubs, clinch the N.L. East flag with one day left in the season as Tudor earns his 20th victory in 21 decisions. The Cardinals win 100 games (101-61) for the first time in 18 years and their 314 stolen bases are the most by any team since 1912. McGee hits .353 to win the batting title. Andujar also wins 21 and **Danny Cox** goes 18-9.

Oct. 14—Ozzie Smith shocks everyone by hitting his first lefthanded homer as a major leaguer, connecting off Dodgers reliever Tom Niedenfuer in the bottom of the ninth inning of Game 5 of the NLCS. The blast gives the Cardinals a 3-2 victory and a 3-2 series lead. The day before, Cardinals rookie speedster Vince Coleman was injured prior to Game 4 when the automatic tarpaulin at Busch Stadium rolled up his leg. Coleman missed the rest of the postseason.

Oct. 16—With a base open and a 5-4 lead in the ninth, Dodgers manager Tommy Lasorda elects to pitch to Clark, who promptly rips a Niedenfuer offering for a three-run homer, giving St. Louis a 7-5 victory and a trip to the World Series.

Oct. 26—The Cardinals suffer perhaps their most heartbreaking World Series defeat—2-1 to the cross-state Royals—as Kansas City rallies for two runs in the ninth inning to win Game 6. A blown call at first by umpire Don Denkinger, a misjudged pop foul by Clark, a passed ball by Porter and a two-run single by Dane Iorg do in the Cards, who then get blasted in Game 7 the next night, 11-0.

Nov. 18—McGee is voted N.L. MVP. Nine days later, Coleman—who steals a rookie-record 110 bases—becomes the fourth unanimous N.L. Rookie of the Year.

1986

Apr. 12—Tudor beats the Expos, 6-3, for his 18th consecutive victory at Busch Stadium.

Aug. 10—Righthander Todd Worrell records his 24th save of the season in a 5-4 victory over the Pirates to set a major league rookie record.

Sept. 15—Mike Laga, batting against the Mets' Ron Darling, achieves a first by hitting a ball completely out of Busch Stadium. One problem: It was a foul ball down the right-field line. Laga struck out on the next pitch.

Oct. 5—The Cardinals fall to 79-82 and finish in third place—28½ games behind the division champion Mets.

Nov. 24—**Worrell** is named N.L. Rookie of the Year.

1987

Apr. 1—The Cardinals acquire catcher Tony Pena from the Pirates for three players, including outfielder Andy Van Slyke.

Apr. 18—Herr makes his first homer of the season a memorable one: a game-winning grand slam off Orosco to beat the Mets, 12-8 in 10 innings, at Busch Stadium. Fans celebrate by heaving the freebies they receive on Seat Cushion Night into the air and onto the field.

Sept. 11—The Cardinals score two runs in the ninth inning

and two more in the 10th for an improbable 6-4 win over the Mets at Shea Stadium. Third baseman Terry Pendleton delivers the biggest blow—a two-run, two-out homer off reliever Roger McDowell in the ninth inning that sends the game into extra innings. The victory gives the struggling Cardinals a 2½-game lead over second-place New York.

Oct. 1—The Cardinals wrap up their third division title in six seasons with an 8-2 victory over the Expos. Three days later, St. Louis, which draws more than three million fans for the first time, ends the season with a 95-67 record.

Oct. 13—Down three games to two in the NLCS, the Cardinals rally to beat the Giants, 1-0, behind Tudor in Game 6. The next night, they win the series as righthander Danny Cox pitches a complete-game victory in Game 7.

Oct. 21—The Cardinals lose a seven-game World Series to Minnesota. The most memorable moment: Game 4, when backup infielder **Tom Lawless** (.080 hitter during the regular season) drives a Frank Viola pitch over the left-field wall at Busch Stadium for only his second homer as a major leaguer. It gives the Cards a 4-1 lead. Lawless then flips his bat nonchalantly in the air, slug-

ger-style, before beginning his home run trot. Lawless' antics send the packed Busch Stadium crowd into a frenzy.

1988

Jan. 6—Clark signs as a free agent with the Yankees.

Jan. 14—The Cardinals sign free agent Bob Horner, a former N.L. Rookie of the Year, as a replacement for Clark.

Apr. 22—The Cardinals trade Herr to the Twins for outfielder Tom Brunansky.

May 14—Infielder Jose Oquendo becomes the first position player to earn a pitching decision in 20 years in a 7-5, 19-inning loss to the Braves.

Aug. 16—The Cardinals trade Tudor to the Dodgers for outfielder **Pedro Guerrero.**

Sept. 24—Oquendo plays catcher in the seventh inning of a game against the Mets to become the first N.L. player since 1918 to play all nine positions in one season.

Oct. 2—At 76-86, the fifth-place Cardinals finish 25 games behind the division champion Mets. Joe Magrane (2.18) becomes the first Cardinal since John Denny in 1976 to lead the league in ERA.

Red Schoendienst

1989

Feb. 28—**Red Schoendienst**, a Cardinal from 1945-56 and 1961-63 and the team's manager from 1965-76, is elected to the Baseball Hall of Fame by the Veterans Committee.

July 28—Coleman has his major league record for consecutive stolen bases end at 50 when he is thrown out by Montreal's Nelson Santovenia in a game at Busch Stadium.

Sept. 8—A three-run homer by Pedro Guerrero is the big blow as the Cardinals rally from a 7-1 deficit to beat the Cubs, 11-8, at Wrigley Field to move to within a half-game of first-place Chicago in the N.L. East. The Cardinals, however, lose their next six games to drop out of the pennant race. They finish the season October 1 in third place at 86-76.

Sept. 29—Owner **August A. Busch Jr.** dies at age 90, and control of the Cardinals falls to Anheuser-Busch brewery executive Fred Kuhlmann.

1990

May 4—The Cardinals trade Brunansky to the Red Sox for closer Lee Smith.

June 29—The Cardinals are no-hit, 6-0, in Los Angeles by Dodgers lefthander Fernando Valenzuela. Earlier that day, Oakland's Dave Stewart throws a 5-0 no-hitter against Toronto, marking the first time in the 20th century that two complete-game no-hitters are pitched on the same day.

TORRE

July 6—Herzog, his team in last place at 33-47, resigns after 10 seasons as manager. Schoendienst assumes the managerial reins on an interim basis.

Aug. 1—**Joe Torre** is hired as manager.

Aug. 29—The Cardinals trade McGee to Oakland for three prospects. McGee, who is hitting .335 at the time of the deal, later is awarded the N.L. batting title even though he has one fewer at-bat than the minimum required, since adding one more at-bat without a hit would not drop his average below that of the second-place hitter, Dodgers first baseman Eddie Murray.

Oct. 3—The Cardinals go 70-92 and finish in last place for the first time since 1918.

1991

Oct. 2—**Lee Smith** records his 47th save of the season in a 6-4 victory over the Expos at Busch Stadium after breaking Sutter's old N.L. record of 45 the day before.

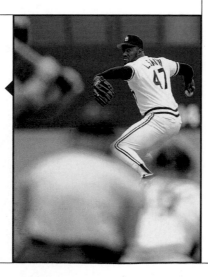

Oct. 6—The Cardinals end the season with a 7-3 loss at Chicago and finish in second place at 84-78.

1992

Apr. 26—Ozzie Smith steals his 500th career base in a 6-0 loss to the Expos at Busch Stadium.

May 26—Ozzie triples in a 5-2 loss to the Dodgers at Busch for career hit No. 2,000.

Sept. 5—Worrell gets career save No. 128 in a 4-0 victory over the Giants to pass Sutter and become the Cardinals' all-time saves leader. The next night, Worrell saves a game for starter Bob Tewksbury, who ends the season with the league's best winning percentage (.762, 16-5), second-best ERA (2.16) and the best walks-per-nine-innings ratio (0.77) of any pitcher since 1933.

Oct. 4—The Cardinals beat the Phillies, 6-3, to finish the season in third place at 83-79.

1993

Apr. 13—Lee Smith passes Jeff Reardon to become baseball's all-time saves leader with No. 358 in a 9-7 victory at Los Angeles.

May 22—Ozzie Smith appears in his 2,223rd game at shortstop, breaking an N.L. record held by Larry Bowa.

Sept. 7—Mark Whiten ties two major league records in the second game of a doubleheader in Cincinnati as he hits four homers and drives in 12 runs in a 15-2 St. Louis victory. His homers are a grand slam in the first inning, three-run blasts in the sixth and seventh innings and a two-run shot in the ninth.

Oct. 3—The Cardinals go 87-75 to finish in third place, 10 games behind N.L. East champion Philadelphia.

1994

May 13-14—Ozzie Smith homers in back-to-back games for the only time in his career.

July 14—**Ozzie** gets his 8,017th career assist to pass Luis Aparicio for the top spot on baseball's all-time list for shortstops.

July 18—The Cardinals tie a National League record by blowing an 11-run lead and losing, 15-12, to the Astros in Houston.

July 30—A crowd of 53,415—the most ever for a regular-season game at Busch Stadium—witness a 10-7 Cardinals win over the Cubs. But there's no pennant on the line—the clubs are tied for fourth place.

Aug. 11—The Cardinals beat the Marlins, 8-6, in Miami in their final game before a players strike wipes out the remainder of the season. The Cardinals finish third in the newly created N.L. Central with a record of 53-61.

1995

June 16—The Cardinals fire Torre after a 20-27 start and trade third baseman Todd Zeile to the Cubs for three players. Farm director Mike Jorgensen takes over as interim manager.
Aug. 10—The Cardinals get a forfeit victory in Los Angeles when Dodgers fans throw that night's promotional give-away—baseballs—on the field.

Oct. 1—The 62-81 Cardinals finish in fourth place in the N.L. Central.

Oct. 23—**Tony La Russa** is hired as manager.

Oct. 25—Anheuser-Busch says it will sell the team and Busch Stadium. Two months later, the Cards are bought by a group of local investors headed by Andrew Baur, Fred Hanser and William DeWitt.

1996

Jan.—Busch Stadium has a grass field for the first time since 1969.

Feb. 13—Dennis Eckersley is obtained in a deal with the A's.

May 18—John Mabry becomes the first Cardinal since Ken Boyer in 1964 to hit for the cycle in order (single, double triple, homer) but Cards lose at Colorado, 9-8.

June 19—Ozzie Smith announces his retirement, effective at the end of the season.
Sept. 24—The Cardinals win their first division title since 1987 as they beat the Pirates, 7-1, to clinch the N.L. Central. Five days later, they end the year at 88-74.

Oct. 5—The Cardinals complete a three-game sweep of the Padres in the N.L. Division Series with a 7-5 victory.

Oct. 13—The Cardinals take a three games-to-one lead over the Braves in the NLCS as they score three runs in the seventh inning of Game 4 to tie the game and then win it, 4-3, on **Brian Jordan**'s solo homer in the eighth inning in St. Louis. The Cardinals, however, lose the next three games by a combined score of 32-1.

1997

Apr. 19—The Cardinals and Padres take major league baseball to Hawaii. The Cards sweep a doubleheader from San Diego, 1-0 and 2-1, in Honolulu.

June 14—St. Louis splits a day-night doubleheader with the Indians at Busch in its first regular-season interleague game.

July 31—The Cardinals acquire first baseman Mark McGwire from Oakland at the trading deadline.

Aug. 8—In his second at-bat at Busch Stadium, McGwire snaps a string of 71 at-bats without a home run by smashing a 441-foot shot off the left-field foul pole against the Phillies. It is McGwire's first National League homer and the 364th of his career.

Sept. 16—McGwire signs a three-year contract extension and celebrates by hitting a 517-foot homer that evening at Busch.

Sept. 28—The Cardinals finish 73-89 and slip to fourth place.

1998

Mar. 31—McGwire hits the first opening-day grand slam in club history in a 6-0 Cardinals win over the Dodgers at Busch Stadium.

Apr. 14—McGwire is the first Cardinal to have a three-homer game at Busch. His spree comes against Arizona.

May 8—McGwire hits his 400th career homer, connecting off the Mets' Rick Reed at Shea Stadium.

May 16—McGwire clubs the longest homer in Busch Stadium history when he tags Florida's Livan Hernandez for a 545-foot shot. The ball just misses landing in the upper deck in center field.

July 26—McGwire breaks Mize's club record for one season with his 44th homer in a 3-1 victory at Colorado.

Sept. 7—McGwire ties Roger Maris' single-season record when he hits home run No. 61 at Busch Stadium off Chicago righthander Mike Morgan—a 430-foot blast that hits off the Stadium Club windows in left field.

Sept. 8—In the fourth inning of a game against the Cubs—the Cardinals' last home game before a five-game road swing—**McGwire** makes history by hitting home run No. 62 to become baseball's single-season home run king. The record-breaker is McGwire's shortest homer of the year—a 341-foot line drive off Cubs righthander Steve Trachsel that barely clears the wall down the left-field line at Busch Stadium. The Cardinals' J.D. Drew makes his major league debut that night and goes 0-for-2.

Sept. 27—McGwire ends his record season by hitting two more homers—his 69th and 70th of the season—on the final day in a 6-3 win over the Expos at Busch Stadium. The Cardinals finish in third place at 83-79. Due mainly to McGwire, they lead the league in homers (223) for the first time since 1944 and reach three million in attendance for the first time since 1989.

1999

Apr. 23—Third baseman **Fernando Tatis** sets a major league record by hitting two grand slams in the same inning in a 12-5 victory at Dodger Stadium. Both come off Chan Ho Park in third inning.

June 25—Rookie Jose Jimenez outduels Randy Johnson—the righthander holds the Diamondbacks hitless and wins, 1-0, in Arizona.

Aug. 5—McGwire hits his 500th career homer, the smash coming against Padres righthander Andy Ashby at Busch Stadium. San Diego's Tony Gwynn, gunning for membership in the 3,000-hit club, ends the game with 2,999.

Oct. 3—The Cardinals close a 75-86 season with a 9-5 win over the Cubs. McGwire finishes the season with 65 homers to lead the majors for a fourth consecutive year.

2000

Apr. 30—McGwire and **Jim Edmonds**—acquired from Anaheim in a March 23 trade—both homer in a 4-3 victory at Philadelphia as the Cardinals end the month with an N.L.-record 55 homers in April.

July 6—After homering in his first major league at-bat two days earlier, Keith McDonald becomes the first N.L. player to homer in his first two career at-bats in a 12-6 loss to Cincinnati.

July 17—Thirteen days after

McDonald homers in his first at-bat, Chris Richard hits the first pitch he sees in the majors (from Twins pitcher Mike Lincoln) over the wall.

July 31—With McGwire injured, the Cardinals acquire veteran first baseman **Will Clark** in a trade with the Orioles.

Sept. 20—The Cardinals clinch their second N.L. Central title in five years with an 11-6 victory over the Astros. St. Louis finishes the season October 1 with a 95-67 record.

Oct. 5—Clark, who hit .345 with 12 homers and 42 RBIs in 171 at-bats

for St. Louis during the regular season, hits a three-run homer in the bottom of the first off Atlanta's Tom Glavine in Game 2 of the Division Series to give the Cardinals a lead they never surrender. The Cards complete a sweep two days later with a 7-1 victory at Atlanta.

Oct. 16—The Mets beat the Cardinals, 7-0, in New York to win the NLCS in five games.

2001

Aug. 11—McGwire hits home run No. 574 off Mets lefthander Glendon Rusch to move past Harmon Killebrew for fifth place on the all-time list.

Aug. 29—The Cardinals beat the Padres, 16-14, in the highest-scoring game in Busch Stadium history.

Sept. 3—Rookie lefthander Bud Smith no-hits the Padres 4-0 in San Diego in his 11th big-league start.

Oct. 4—McGwire hits the 583rd and final homer of his career off the Brewers' Rocky Coppinger in a 10-3 St. Louis win at Milwaukee.

Oct. 7—The Cardinals close the season with a 9-2 loss to the Astros at Busch Stadium to finish tied with Houston in the N.L. Central at 93-69. Because Houston won the season series with St. Louis, the Cardinals qualify for the playoffs as the N.L. wild card.

Oct. 15—The Cardinals are knocked out of the playoffs when Arizona's Tony Womack delivers an RBI single in the bottom of the ninth to beat St. Louis, 2-1, in Game 5 of the Division Series.

Nov. 11—McGwire announces his retirement.

▶ **Nov. 12**— Outfielder/third baseman/first baseman **Albert Pujols** (.329, 37 homers, 130 RBIs) is unanimously voted N.L. Rookie of the Year. RBI total is a National League record for a rookie.

2002

Jan. 8—**Ozzie Smith**, a Cardinal from 1982-96, is elected to the Baseball Hall of Fame.